Mindful Cricket.

How to create the mindset
you need to be the best
cricketer you can be

To Carol, Ben, Mark, Kate and Leo

A catalogue record for this book is available from the National Library of Australia

NATIONAL LIBRARY OF AUSTRALIA

www.mindfulcricket.com

Winter, Graham (author)
Mindful Cricket
ISBN (paper back) 978-1-922337-99-3
ISBN (eBook) 978-1-922337-19-1

Typeset Expo Serif 10/16
Internal images by Claire Magarey (*Somersault Design*)
Cover and book design by Green Hill Publishing

Contents.

About The Author.

Graham Winter played first class cricket before retiring early to pursue a career as a performance psychologist.

From winning Sheffield Shield and One Day Cup Teams, he stepped into a varied and high-profile career as the performance psychology coach to Olympic gold medallists, test cricketers and the executive teams of international corporations.

Career highlights include, three times Chief Psychologist to the Australian Olympic Team, Consultant to the ICC Academy and Australian Test Cricket Team, Advisor / Designer with PwC's Asia Pacific Strategic Change Practice and Founder of Consulting firm Think One Team Consulting (www. thinkoneteam.com).

Graham is the best-selling author of five books published by John Wiley, including *Think One Team*, *High Performance Leadership*, and *First Be Nimble*.

In *Mindful Cricket* he brings together his unique experiences and passion for performance psychology and cricket to challenge and equip cricketers and coaches to find better ways to play a sport which everyone knows is played above the shoulders.

Acknowledgements.

Writing a book isn't a simple project with a start and finish. This book, more than any other I've authored has been decades in the making. It is the weaving of experiences across a lifetime of playing, watching, and coaching cricket and enjoying remarkably diverse professional experiences all tied together by a curiosity and passion to better understand and enhance the link between psychology and performance.

My earliest childhood memories include tossing hard rubber balls against the neighbours' garage wall as I waited for Dad to get home from work so we could play a game of cricket. Those balls and the harder ones that followed smashed more than a few windows, dented cars, fences and sheds, and sent my sister Helen scurrying for cover. Fortunately, Mum and Dad saw my passion for cricket and their love, support and hard work shaped those early years.

Perhaps the greatest sadness of my life is that Dad died before I graduated from University or played First Class Cricket. He put in but as a teenager I didn't give back, but the ripples of his life live on in our family and in my own role as a father and mentor.

In the same year my Dad passed away, I met Carol who became my wife, the love of my life and partner in raising our wonderful sons Mark and Ben. Fortunately, Carol carried on the family tradition of driving boys to cricket and turning a blind eye to anything broken by a cricket ball or by the occasional ill-considered practice swing with a bat in the lounge room. We wait expectantly to see if Leo, our grandson gives our daughter-in-law Kate the same challenges and opportunities.

In cricket it is friendships and mateships which last. For that I'm grateful to my two Grade clubs, Adelaide University and Prospect, and the South

Australian Cricket Association for giving me the chance to play with and against many wonderful players.

Coaches play a pivotal role in cricket and I was fortunate to have the late Chester Bennett as my coach through school and later in club cricket. His gentle manner, considered wisdom, and belief in human potential shaped me and many young cricketers into better players and better people.

In a career as a performance psychologist spanning both elite sport and business across more than thirty years there are just too many people to acknowledge, however I want to thank the almost countless colleagues and clients who have trusted, supported and challenged me to be the best I can be. When I reflect on the opportunities to consult to companies and work with Olympic champions across almost every continent, I realise how much trust people have placed in me and for that I am extremely grateful.

And so, to those who have had a direct hand in the past year to bring this book and the associated programs to life:

Kylie Smith my indispensable Assistant, Coordinator, Organiser and Encourager. Without Kylie's belief, energy and insistence on staying the course this book might never have landed. So committed is Kylie that not once but twice her parents Tony and Val Smith bundled up and moved our offices while I kept clicking away on the computer. They have a delightful and talented daughter and I greatly appreciate their generosity in helping me to make this possible.

Silvana Marveggio worked tirelessly to keep the manuscript moving along while we balanced the ever-present business consulting load. Her understanding as our priorities shifted made it so much easier to navigate the challenges of change. Alfredo Cabada joined us late in the writing process and is playing a vital role in creating the all-important resources and tools for the Mindful Cricket community.

I've been fortunate during the drafting of Mindful Cricket to have a network of cricket coaches and former players who generously provided feedback and ideas to shape my thinking and the evolving manuscript.

Ashley Ross, Peter Spence, Ron Steiner and Toot Byron have time and again given up their time to speak with me, to share ideas and to read and deeply reflect on how to make this more effective. Ashley, your vision and commitment to find better ways to develop the mindset of cricketers around the world was the spark that started the fire. Peter, your depth of understanding of mindfulness, your care and attention to detail and willingness to challenge my thinking helped enormously as I battled with some of the complexity of this topic. Ron, as ever you told me the truth and are generous beyond measure. Toot, you are an inspiration and ahead of your time, but I hope it's arriving now!

Insightful feedback and ideas from Malcolm Dolman, Grant Wyman, Daniel Sutton, Brian McFadyen, Peter Clarke, Tom Rutherford, Mark Winter, Tim Dansie, Greg Shipperd, Andrew Zesers and Shaun Seigert regularly helped me to create a program suited to cricketers and their coaches.

Brett Penno has been brilliant in creating the framework for the website, Claire Magarey yet again met our needs for graphic design, and the team at Green Hill Publishing led by David and Gina Walters, and expertly guided by Senior Editor Lisa Lark and Nicola Day who brought the book to life.

Finally, a big thank you to all my colleagues and friends for giving me the belief and support to create a book which I am proud to offer to the cricketing world as a small payback for all the cricketing world has given to me.

Introduction.

This is not a book about how to bowl or hit a cricket ball. A book like that would teach you technical skills, which are important, but they're not what makes a successful cricketer.

Every outstanding cricketer understands that cricket is played above the shoulders. The mind is the secret to playing better cricket, and yet cricket has a serious problem. Our traditional approach to practice, training and playing the game leaves players ill-equipped to master the mental game of cricket.

What follows is a four-part framework which addresses that problem in a way that has the potential to change the way you think about cricket and how you practise and play the game. From my first cricket match at the age of nine, to my First Class debut on the Western Australian Cricket Association (WACA) and in games against the West Indies and Pakistan, during my professional career as Chief Psychologist to the Australian Olympic Team, and when consulting to dozens of global businesses and sports teams across Asia, the Middle East and US, I have seen this framework transform the results and enjoyment people get from sport and from life. It is built on proven practices of mindfulness and performance psychology and will work for you regardless of your level as a cricketer or coach, because it builds a foundation for life, and then applies it to your cricket and beyond.

To get the most from this book, I encourage you to take three actions:

1. **Decide whether you want to dip, swim or deep dive into this topic,** because this is a playbook and there is lots of information. To dip, just flick and find interesting stuff; to swim, follow the flow of the book; and if you choose to deep dive, read at least to the end of the Clear Mind section before you take action, because the learning loops will be your "operating rhythm."

2. **Join the Mindful Cricket community at** www.mindfulcricket.com so you have immediate access to the activities, guides and tools you'll need to apply the principles and practices.

3. **Purchase the Mindful Cricket Workbook** which is designed as a supplement to this book and as a practical way to introduce Game Mindset to players.

Cricket has changed and continues to evolve. Technique isn't enough. Players who develop their mindset grow with the game, and they are the players who don't get left behind. Let's all enjoy the great sport of cricket and reap the rewards from learning how to play the game above the shoulders.

Note to Coaches.

This Mindful Cricket book is targeted at the serious cricketer and coach. However, as you'll see, it speaks to the player rather than the coach. That's intentional because, even though you play the vital role in creating the learning environment, it is the player's mindset that is key to growth in performance.

A number of highly experienced coaches have helped me to construct this book and the associated Workbook. We all agreed that the modern cricket coach will appreciate this format because it provides lots of ideas and activities to support the coaching process, while setting up the expectation that players are ultimately responsible for their own learning and development.

I hope you enjoy the book and I look forward to engaging with you through www.mindfulcricket.com and Mindful Cricket community.

Game Mindset Model.

Clear Mind.

Composed

Focused

Simple

Adapt fast

Play Brave.

Bold Vision

Put it on the Line

Hold the Tension

Play Clever.

Bat Smart

Bowl Smart

Keep & Field Smart

Play Better.

Growth Mindset

Be Game Ready

Bring Optimism

Part A.

THE GAME ABOVE THE SHOULDERS.

CHAPTER 1

Why Technique Is Overrated.

Cricket is played above the shoulders. We all know this because, sometimes we can play well one day and then poorly the next. Our basic ability to bat, bowl, keep and field doesn't change, but form comes and goes like clouds on a windy day, so we do what cricketers have always done. We spend hours in the nets working on technique, timing and rhythm, only to end up even more frustrated when still playing poorly.

We ask coaches if the problem could be something else in our technique or, worse still, we ask ourselves if we're just not talented enough. But what if the problem isn't technique or talent? What if the problem is the way we think about the game itself?

The Difference is Mindset.

The problem is simple. Even the best players have flaws in their techniques - just look at Steve Smith or Jasprit Bumrah. And yet, despite those flaws, they score runs and take wickets on a regular basis in all forms of the game.

The fact is, technique and talent are overrated. It is clear that confident composed minds make runs and take wickets. Filling your mind with thoughts about technique or striving to get better won't help if you don't start with the right mindset. Go to the nets with the wrong mindset and you'll grip the bat too tight, meet high catches with hard hands, and lose bowling rhythm by trying too hard.

Still, finding the right mindset isn't easy. An emerging Test player once told me that at times he felt as if he couldn't hit the ball off the wicket square no matter how hard he tried. I understand. In my first few limited overs matches, I couldn't swing the white ball despite that being my greatest strength with a red ball.

Like the Test player, I was full of self-doubt and frustration until I began working as a psychologist with Olympic champions and international cricketers. I studied the differences between those who did consistently well in moments that matter, and those who didn't, and found that the differences were rarely physical. Time and again I observed that the winners were calmer in mind, quietly confident, and clever in their decision making, while others seemed to be working harder but lacking the poise and balance to be at their best.

The difference was mindset.

Mindfulness and Game Mindset.

It's obvious, really. We play our best cricket - or do our best at anything - when we are mindful, which means our mind is clear, composed and fully focused on the challenges of the moment. However, we don't play so well when preoccupied with complicated thoughts, or distracted by impatience, self-doubt or even over-confidence.

This awareness of the power of "mindfulness" has led many top athletes and teams around the world (from NBA stars, to Wimbledon champions and Olympic medallists) to embrace mindfulness practices as an integral part of their training and development as athletes and people. Those practices develop the sort of patience and composure needed by cricketers, but the big question is: How can we make mindful practices relevant and practical for cricketers and cricket coaches so the benefits flow into our great game?

This question led me to create a **four-step framework** based on my personal experiences as a performance psychologist and first-class cricketer, to help cricketers and coaches find and develop this mindful approach in sport and life. I called the approach **Game Mindset**. When the Test player learned and applied this approach, he said that the game seemed easier. His performances became more consistent, and by the end of his career he was an international star with an average near fifty.

Game Mindset isn't complicated or contrived. Quite the opposite. It's a way of thinking and a suite of practices, activities, drills and tools built on mindfulness and performance psychology principles designed to help you enjoy your cricket and be the best cricketer you can be.

Your Learning Pathway.

Welcome to the fast-growing community of Mindful Cricketers and coaches around the world! Your journey begins with this book and the ever-expanding suite of Mindful Cricket resources available through the website www.mindfulcricket.com.

In this book you will explore and understand the unique challenges of the game of cricket and why so much of it is played above the shoulders. Then you'll learn how to identify, develop and hone your own unique Game Mindset for whatever level or form of the game you are playing. It doesn't matter if that is Test cricket or 20/20, club or courtyard, or school cricket and beach cricket.

Let's now explore and understand a bit more about the challenges presented by the game of cricket, so you can enjoy the game and play better cricket.

Mindful Cricket is about embracing the practices of mindfulness and applying activities, drills and tools to become the best cricketer (and person) you can be.

CHAPTER 2

Why Cricket Is Played Above The Shoulders.

Whether batting, bowling, wicket-keeping or fielding, the game of cricket presents many unique challenges and opportunities. Understanding these challenges and their implications for the way you think, act and feel will help you to appreciate why developing a Game Mindset can lead to better cricket.

Before doing that, it is important to call out one of the biggest challenges we face in cricket: the difference between the practice environment (the nets) and the match environment. While golfers practise and play on courses, tennis players on courts and footballers on fields, cricketers are left to learn to play in an alleyway of net or wire, which is very different to the match conditions.

You would think this would force the sport of cricket to find more innovative ways to practise the game (and the required mindset) but it seems almost the opposite, and only forward-thinking coaches have been open to finding new and better ways. These coaches are acutely aware that mindset can make or break performance and enjoyment, and they design practice to help players go beyond just working on technical skills and to learn how to prepare for and succeed in the face of the mental challenges.

We explore those challenges in this Chapter, and then throughout the book we look at how to set up your practice environment and ways of playing, in order to learn not just the technical skills but how to play the mind game.

Mindful Batting.

Is there one aspect of the game more influenced by mindset than any other? If there is, it is likely to be batting. Here are some reasons for that.

The Challenges of the Game.

Batting presents a host of challenges, and one looms larger in the mind than anything else: instant dismissal. Even talented international players fear the dreaded "duck" and succumb to nerves early in their innings. Unfortunately, some never learn how to train their minds to bring the composure and focus that will help them navigate the early part of the innings.

Few sports penalise players as harshly as cricket punishes the batsman. Can you imagine a tennis player missing their first serve and being told by the umpire that their day is over? On the positive side, few sports let you control the game for hours while eleven eager opponents chase balls over a very large field!

Mindful Cricket is a way of getting through the fear of failure by focusing on what's important and getting on with building an innings.

This mindset of accepting things as they are, and letting go of fears and worries, helps batsmen master two other challenges: position in the batting order and adapting to different pitches and conditions.

Position in the batting order can make a big difference for some players and not at all for others. Is that more evidence for the power of mindset over technique and talent? Facing the new ball bowlers when they are fresh requires quick reactions, good judgement of line and length, and courage to handle physical intimidation. Middle order challenges are many and varied. Coming in after a quick collapse is vastly different to following a big partnership. Every position from one to eleven has its own demands and rewards, and even these change from innings to innings.

Adapting to different conditions begins on arrival at the crease. Light, pitch, bowling and opposing team all play a part, and the opposing captain will do their best to keep you off balance.

The Inner Game of Batting.

The game has plenty of challenges, but the key is the mindset you bring to them.

REFLECTION QUESTIONS

What is the mindset you bring to the crease?

Are you more focused on playing positively or avoiding being dismissed?

How do emotions help or hinder your decision making?

Is your mind clear or confused?

Is your batting routine simple and repeatable?

Can you maintain concentration over a long innings?

Does your reflection on these questions suggest you might be missing out on runs because of mindset?

Why Mindset Fails Batsmen.

To understand the inner game of batting, I've studied the behaviours and practices of cricketers and spoken with many successful coaches. Three reasons seem fundamental to whether mindset helps or hinders enjoyment and performance: Feelings, Focus and Self-Belief.

FEELINGS such as nervousness and frustration play a part in the outcome of most matches and are the reason that "Cultivate Composure" is a foundation principle in Mindful Cricket. Feeling nervous while waiting to bat or early in your innings is your mind's natural response to a challenge. It's called the flight-or-fight response, and it's wired into your brain and nervous system to sharpen focus and response to threats.

Reflect on your approach to batting early in your innings. Do you get the balance right between "flight" (being too tentative) and "fight" (impulsive or rash shots)? **Mindful Cricket practices can help you to find the balance between "fight" and "flight" by reducing the unhelpful fear of failure.**

Another feeling or emotion that brings batsmen undone is frustration, which every bowler understands and welcomes, because on a flat pitch or in a 20/20 match the plan is often to "dry up" the runs and trigger a rash shot.

Has frustration got the better of you when you are not scoring as quickly as the team needs, or a poor bowler has you pinned down? **Mindful practices can reduce impatience and tone down the causes of frustration.**

FOCUS is a key to successful batting. An average batsman with good concentration and reasonable technique often outscores more talented teammates who can't control their concentration. Bowlers might get away with attention lapses, but if a batsman loses focus for just one ball, they might be heading back to the grandstand.

Our minds aren't naturally conditioned to focus in the way that is needed for batting. We are "scanners" who like to observe what's going on around us rather than just what's essential, and we're "dreamers" who flick attention from the past to the future and back again.

Mindful Cricket activities and drills will show you how to train your mind to focus on what's essential, and to be less distracted by things which don't matter - including the ball you just played and missed, or that half century you are imagining. Any improvement in your ability to focus calmly and confidently in the present moment is a sure way to boost consistency and results in cricket and other areas of your life.

SELF BELIEF can be the difference between succeeding in big moments and being left disappointed. With self-belief, we put ourselves out there amongst the challenges, and take intelligent risks along the way. Without self-belief we hesitate, play more conservatively, and try to avoid failing.

Did you know that a boost in self-belief often starts with being less self-critical? One reason for this is that cricketers can be perfectionists who set impossibly high standards, notice all their own mistakes, under-value their achievements, and then get more disappointed with their performance. Ironically, their skills and results are usually getting better, but it's never good enough for them. Is this a pattern you recognise in yourself or teammates?

Why Mindful Batting is the Answer.

There are two "mental errors" which often cause batsmen disappointment. First, they bring to the game a *Don't get out* mindset, which causes them to tighten their grip on the bat, move tentatively and create the very conditions where their greatest fear is most likely to come true. Second, they lose their focus in the moment (what is), and instead think about what just happened, or what might happen in the future (what if). Bowlers love it when batsmen aren't fully concentrating because they overhit a slower ball, misjudge the length, or fail to see the fielder move into position to catch what seemed a perfectly safe hook shot.

Mindful batting avoids these errors by playing each bowler and each delivery on merit. It is trusting in your preparation, and trusting in yourself to make the right decision, rather than premeditating on whether the next ball is a bouncer or a half volley.

Mindful batsmen don't let what happened to the previous ball distract their focus on this one; they enjoy the high stakes situations when pressure is getting to other players, and they calmly deal with comments from fielders and distractions at the ground.

It's so simple. Mindful batting means you are doing the mental and physical preparation and trusting yourself to play the game one ball at a time. It is the mindset to be the best you can be.

Mindful Bowling.

Bowling can be fast, slow or any variation of swing, seam and spin in between. Every piece of cricket action starts with the bowler delivering the ball. As a bowler you have the first opportunity to influence what happens in a match, which is a strong hint that mindset plays a key part in game tactics and strategies.

Need a second hint? How about the laws of the game being heavily weighted in the batsman's favour? Benefit of the doubt, no leg side LBWs, ropes for shorter boundaries, and the ever controversial and contradictory rules around ball polishing versus tampering - is there any doubt Cricket's governing bodies want to make things easier for batsmen?

Here are some other reasons why mindset plays a key part in bowling.

The Challenges of the Game.

Bowling has its challenges, starting with the physical demands which cause fatigued bowlers to lose their line and length. Long spells, hot or cold conditions, and bowling into strong winds all play a part in this; and then there are the short form matches, where bowling single overs in separate spells means being physically and mentally ready from the first ball.

Another challenge for bowlers is that "effort for outcome" is just not fair. Your best effort in most sports produces your best result. Not in cricket. Your best ball can be hit for six, the pitch can be so flat that even the most perfect leg break doesn't catch the edge of the bat, and other bowlers take wickets bowling rubbish while your best deliveries just beat the bat.

Bowling can be exciting, satisfying, tedious or even downright frustrating. However, mindful bowling is about persisting and exerting pressure. It does not mean expecting a wicket every ball. Small rewards come from shaping the way the batsman plays and believing persistence will be rewarded because even the greatest Test bowlers of all time average less than one wicket every fifty deliveries.

Every type of bowling has its own unique challenges. Bowling fast is most cricketer's dream, but few achieve true express pace. Fast bowlers must learn to handle the physical demands on their bodies, while finding rhythm and control of line and length at full pace.

Medium pace bowling is more a battle of tactics. While a fast bowler blasts out the batsman, the medium pacer's weapons of choice are movement in the air and off the pitch, and variations in line, length and pace.

Spin bowling is the most subtle art in cricket, and arguably the most mentally demanding. Slow bowlers don't have the luxury of straying in line and length to the same extent as quicker bowlers. The margin for error is small, so the challenge is to relax and employ the sort of subtle control more often seen in sports like golf and bowls. Short form cricket was expected to be the death of spinners, but the opposite has come true. Wrist spinners dominate the top bowler lists in 20/20 competitions. How? Mostly by pushing the ball through quickly, and relying less on deceiving the batsman in flight, and more on hitting a difficult length where a little sideways spin causes uncertainty.

Whether your speciality is fast, medium pace or slow, the physical and technical challenges are obvious. However, as with batting, it is mindset - feelings, focus and self-belief - that is likely to make or break success.

The Inner Game of Bowling.

REFLECTION QUESTIONS

How effectively do you bowl when under pressure?

Are you more inclined to enjoy the challenge of working out a batsmen's weaknesses, or do you just go all out for a wicket every ball?

How do emotions help or hinder your bowling?

Can you keep composure and rhythm when the batsmen are in control?

Is your bowling routine simple and repeatable?

Do you keep a clear and clever mind?

How many wickets are you missing out on because you lose belief, focus and control when things aren't going well for you?

Why Mindset Fails Bowlers.

Feelings, focus and self-belief affect bowlers as much as batsmen, but there are subtle differences which come into play.

FEELINGS such as excessive tension or fatigue are common causes of poor bowling. Tension destroys rhythm and there's nothing more important to bowling than rhythm. With rhythm, you bowl faster with less effort, get more flight and turn, swing the ball later, and find that extra zip off the pitch.

Tension starts when a bowler's mind starts to wonder: What if the next ball goes for six? What if I bowl a full toss? Why is this pitch so flat? Will this umpire ever give an LBW?

And cricketers' minds don't just speculate about what might happen, they're just as good at dredging up the past. Everyone drops catches (and has them dropped off their own bowling), and everyone bowls poor deliveries and gets slogged, but dwelling in the past just creates more frustration or anxiety and distraction.

This highlights a crucial principle of Mindful Cricket: It's not the first setback that will cost you, but letting it distract you, so it causes another one. **Mindful Cricket is finding and maintaining rhythm in your bowling by reducing tension and trusting yourself to be your best in moments that matter.**

Another feeling that needs a mention is fatigue or tiredness, because in hot conditions or long spells in the field, the mind often gives up before the body does. Have you let tiredness or fatigue affect your bowling when you've come back late in the day, or been asked to push up into a strong wind for over after over? Maybe a boost in fitness is needed - but if you've ever felt that way, and then got an energy boost from a surprise wicket, you'll know you have more to give.

FOCUS doesn't immediately seem as important for bowlers as it does for batsmen; however, it is a different style of focus that will bring out the best bowling performances. Clever bowlers don't mindlessly run in and deliver the ball. They have plans. They're like scientists running continual experiments. In the nets, in games and even in the backyard, they observe the batsman and the conditions, conceive a plan, and then test it.

What do you observe about a batsman? Do they prefer front or back foot, offside or onside? Is their bat straight or angled in defence? Do they play hard at the ball or let it come to them? How do they respond to a maiden over?

Mindful Cricket is learning to read the game and win the mental battle with batsmen.

SELF-BELIEF shows in bowlers' grit, determination and persistence in keeping on running in and executing their plan. Lack of self-belief causes bowlers to lose energy, to stop applying pressure on the batsman, and to give up.

Self-belief starts with putting in the work at training, and then it is sustained by an optimistic mindset. In a nutshell, an optimist believes they can make something of a situation, and a pessimist doesn't. You can learn to be more optimistic. **Mindful Cricket practices will help you to quieten that self-critical voice that says it's too hard or you're not good enough.**

. . . .

Why Mindful Bowling is the Answer.

Two "mental errors" often cause bowlers disappointment.

The first is trying too hard, which means they run in faster, grip the ball tighter and lose the rhythm that is key to all types of bowling. It's a natural reaction, but it's a vicious circle because without rhythm there is less control and zip, and less flight or turn, which just adds to the pressure.

The second mental error is not having a clear and simple plan. Sometimes the conditions are so good the bowler expects the pitch to do the work, or perhaps the batsmen are set on a flat pitch and a plan seems worthless. Bowlers have first option to control the tempo of the game; however, when batsmen control the tempo, it's a sure sign they're winning the mental game.

Mindful bowling is having a plan and finding a relaxed and confident rhythm. It is preparing well, observing carefully and subtly pressuring the batsman. It is persisting instead of allowing the conditions, or what happened to the previous ball, to affect your focus on executing the plan. It is knowing when to relax, and how to keep it simple and enjoy the challenge.

It's so simple. Mindful bowling is doing the mental and physical preparation, so you can enjoy the challenge of unsettling and ultimately dismissing the batsman. It is setting up for success.

Mindful Wicket-Keeping.

A typical cricket team is made up of five specialist batsmen, one all-rounder, four bowlers, and one wicket-keeper. Traditionally, that has meant the fourth-best batsman in the club plays A grade, while the fourth-best wicket-keeper plays D grade.

The outstanding success of wicket-keeper batsmen like Adam Gilchrist, Jonny Bairstow and Alyssa Healy has transformed the expectations, roles and skills of wicket-keepers. In fact, many first-class teams have two or three batsmen who are all competent keepers.

Like all cricket activities, keeping has high points, like taking a diving catch, and low points, such as missing an easy stumping. Mindful keepers focus when the bowler runs in and remain fully alert until the ball has been played and is dead. We take it for granted that they will pick the spinner's wrong 'un, stop wide balls down the leg side, pick up the low catches that fall in front of the slips, and sprint to the stumps whenever a run is taken.

In many ways, the mental demands for the keeper are a mix of those for batting and bowling, because there are intense physical demands as well as the need for ball-by-ball concentration and maintaining a high standard of balance, movement and timing.

Wicket-keepers play a vital team role not just in taking catches and making stumpings, but also in setting standards, energy and tempo in the field. With the right mindset the keeper is not only boosting their own game but also creating the centre point for focus and energy on the field.

Mindful Fielding.

Great fieldsmen turn matches with their catching, ground fielding and throwing skills, and good fielding is often the difference between winning and losing. The "almost catch" by Herschelle Gibbs in the 1999 World Cup is perhaps the most infamous. As an aside, how many people remember that match for the catch Gibbs let slip while excitedly throwing it up, or for the 101 he scored?

A team of average bowlers supported by energetic fielders, who grab half chances and excel in ground fielding, can pressure strong batting sides and create opportunities which turn matches. On the flip side, dropping catches and giving away easy runs can demoralise bowlers and make it so much more difficult to win.

Arguably the biggest mindset mistake for fielders is lack of interest in the task itself. Poor fielders bring little energy or attention; but the best fielders have a positive attitude, do lots of practice, and know how to switch concentration on and off. They set themselves high standards on the field and want the ball to be hit to them, as they plot ways to run out the batsmen.

The ability to switch concentration on and off has a lot to do with routines or rituals. Some players like to chat between deliveries, and others will walk back to the marked spot and then move in quickly as the bowler begins their run. The key is to be alert for catches and opportunities to impact the play by cutting off runs or creating run outs.

Fielders, like wicket-keepers, can have their confidence shattered if they drop a catch. If this happens to you, put it behind you and get on with making the most of the next opportunity.

Applying a mindful approach to your fielding can help you to make an even bigger contribution to the team.

Key Point Summary.

- Mindful Cricket begins with understanding the challenges of the game and the role of mindset in successfully meeting these challenges.
- Cricket practice is a very different environment from a match, so we need better ways to equip players to play the mental game.
- How you handle feelings, focus and self-belief is likely to make or break the enjoyment and results you get from cricket.
- Batting has the very real chance of instant dismissal and requires adapting to position in the order and to different bowlers and conditions. Mindful batting begins by accepting and embracing these as part of the game.
- Nervousness and frustration derail batsmen, along with the fear of failure and loss of focus on what's happening in the moment.

Mindful practices can build calmness, composure and concentration to take it on one ball at a time.

- Bowling is physically demanding and unpredictable, with rules weighted in the batsman's favour. For this reason, mindful bowling begins by accepting and embracing these as some of the challenges of the game to overcome.
- Too much tension destroys rhythm, which causes bowlers to lose their line, length and "zip", just as fatigue and distraction take away energy. Mindful practices help bowlers to create opportunities by sticking to their plans and absorbing and applying pressure.
- Wicket-keeping and fielding each have their own challenges and requirements for a mindset of focus, energy and teamwork.
- Cricket has many unique challenges, which mindful players accept and enjoy. That is why they are successful in playing the game above the shoulders.

Feelings, Focus and Self-Belief are themes we visit time and again in Mindful Cricket. If you have identified areas where you'd like to improve, then you'll find plenty of practical ideas and tools in this book, and the online resources to make those changes.

Next, we pull together the insights from this chapter and show you how they've been used to create the centrepiece of Mindful Cricket - the Game Mindset.

CHAPTER 3

Mindset To The Rescue.

Is cricket a simple game or a complicated game? It depends who you ask, because players who are out of form and overwhelmed by challenges tend to say it's complicated, while those scoring runs and taking wickets see it as simple.

They can't both be right - or perhaps they can. We all confront four enemies in batting, bowling, keeping, fielding, and in our general lives, which can make almost anything seem difficult and overwhelming. When you understand these enemies and their impact on the challenges of the game of cricket as discussed in the previous chapter, you'll see how and why developing your own unique Game Mindset can be so powerful.

Clarity is the Key.

Imagine you are driving through the busy, jumbled streets of Mumbai.

Where do you focus your attention? How do you navigate the endlessly changing streetscape? Could you plan your way through every metre of the journey? And imagine what would happen if you turned to gesture angrily at the driver who just cut you off?

Exactly! You'd crash, and soon decide it was impossible to drive in Mumbai. You might be right. But good Mumbai drivers bring a special type of mindset - a clear mind. They're composed and alert, focused in the moment, scanning for upcoming risks and opportunities, and ready to adapt to whatever happens. It's as if they hold control of a very small space around them.

And so it is in cricket. When the ball is delivered, clear-minded batsmen are poised, focused in the moment and ready to adapt. Clear-minded bowlers stick to their routines and rituals, and their rhythm and plans, without letting a lucky shot upset their focus and confidence. Clear-minded captains make the right calls; clear-minded keepers and fielders catch with soft hands and throw down stumps; and clear-minded umpires make accurate decisions.

Before we deep dive into how to create a Clear Mind, it is important to call out the four enemies which muddy a Clear Mind and derail everyone from Mumbai taxi drivers to teams of cricketers.

Enemy 1: A Reactive Mind.

The first enemy is letting the mind become so reactive that you lose composure and let unhelpful and uncomfortable emotions take over. The great cricket stories are about players who succeed despite unpredictable pitches, intimidating opponents or seemingly hopeless game positions. It isn't about responding cleverly but about winning the battle over the uncomfortable emotions and the temptation to react emotionally. You've seen it often in the final overs of big games when composed bowlers or batsmen win the game for their team, while their opponents let emotions get the better of them.

Without composure, bowlers lose rhythm, batsmen lose judgement and fielders lose touch. Mistimed shots, erratic bowling and dropped catches are rarely caused by poor technique or talent, but rather by loss of composure.

Enemy 2: Distraction and Mind Drift.

The second enemy is letting the mind be distracted. Cricket demands clear focus on what matters in the present moment. Whether batting, bowling, fielding or keeping, it's a game played one ball at a time, yet our minds don't necessarily work like that. The poor umpiring decision, the play and miss, the dropped catch and the likelihood of winning or losing all create mind drift away from here and now.

Without focus in the present, batsmen miss cues from bowlers and fail to really watch the ball, while bowlers struggle for the consistency of line and length which is always the recipe for success.

Enemy 3: Making it Complicated.

The third enemy is making it complicated rather than keeping it simple.

Of course, we're wired to react to threats and opportunities, so it's no surprise that it's difficult to keep things simple, particularly in the moments that matter. With the best of intentions, we overthink by trying to control all that's happening. Add that to the advice from well-meaning team-mates or observers, and things become so complicated we forget the basics that matter!

Imagine that a team needs eight runs to win at the start of the last over of a 20/20 final. The mindful player is composed, weighs up the best scoring options and then settles with relaxed aggression, waiting on the bowler. With timing and placement, they easily pick off the runs in twos.

What a contrast to the player who, thinking they must hit a boundary, swings hard at the first ball, lifts their eyes too early, and drags the ball waist-high to mid-wicket, leaving a new batsman with an even tougher challenge.

Enemy 4: Slow to Change.

The fourth enemy is being slow and inflexible about learning and adapting to change. Cricket is constantly changing. No two pitches are the same, all bowlers are different, and even balls that look the same behave differently. The game changes in an instant with a dropped catch, two quick wickets or even lucky edges through slips.

You can't play cricket successfully without the ability to adapt to the conditions and the game itself. It is a conservative game with many traditions and myths that restrict and even work against players and coaches learning and adapting fast. Without the mindset and skills to quickly learn and adapt, batsmen misjudge the pace of the pitch, keepers let through countless byes and bowlers serve deliveries right into the batsman's strengths. That's no way to play a game that is constantly changing.

REFLECTION QUESTIONS

To what extent do these four enemies affect your game and your wider life?

Do you maintain poise and composure in the moments that matter, or do you let uncomfortable feelings like nervousness and frustration take over?

Is being focused in the moment easy to do, or does your mind drift to what happened to the ball before or what might happen in the future?

Do you naturally keep things simple and uncomplicated, or do you tend to overthink or get a scrambled mind when there's a lot happening?

How quickly can you adapt to different pitches and forms of the game, and to the rapidly shifting tactics that emerge during a match?

If any of these enemies seem familiar, that's entirely expected because they are universal enemies to which we are all susceptible. The good news is you can learn to do something about it.

A Simple Insight.

On the flipside of these four enemies sits a brilliantly clear insight: we play better when composed, focused in the moment, keeping it simple, and adapting fast.

Think again about your own game and how clarity of mind affects how you tap your talent and technique.

Whether you are playing international, club, school or courtyard cricket, an unclear mind can cost you runs, wickets and enjoyment, whereas a Clear Mind will bring you back to what you do best.

My debut game was on the WACA against a Western Australian team including Dennis Lillee and Terry Alderman, two of the greatest outswing bowlers of all time. My speciality was outswing, and I am always indebted to John Inverarity, who reminded me that we were all chosen because we're good Club cricketers. His simple message was, "Bowl the stuff that got you selected", and I'm pleased to say I took five wickets in that first innings by keeping things simple, being me and not copying my heroes. (I also found Dennis and Terry extremely generous in sharing ideas that I took back to practise and bring into my game.)

How often have you let things get complicated instead of just doing what you do best? Have bowlers pressured you into making mistakes, or did you put pressure on yourself and play the big shot once too often? Have you realised too late that it was time to adapt and change your tactics? How often have you been dismissed by your own poor concentration? When did you last drop an easy catch because you were worried about dropping it?

A Simple Formula.

Are you frustrated, or optimistic that there's more to your game? More runs, wickets, catches and fun?

Things can be different. Things can be better. For this to happen consistently, you need a formula - a simple, reliable formula which clears the mind, embraces the challenge and helps you to master the game in even the toughest of circumstances. A formula can give you a path to follow, and to come back to whenever you sense you are off track, just as good coaches give you technical formulas for batting, bowling and keeping.

That formula is **your unique Game Mindset**. Let's identify, develop and hone it so you can play Mindful Cricket.

Key Point Summary.

- · We all confront four enemies in batting, bowling, keeping, fielding, and in our general lives, which can make almost anything seem difficult and overwhelming.

- On the flipside of the four enemies sits a brilliantly clear insight: we play better when composed, focused in the moment, keeping it simple, and adapting fast.
- When the ball is delivered, clear-minded batsmen are still, poised, focused in the moment and ready to adapt.
- Clear-minded bowlers stick to their routines and rituals, and their rhythm and plans, without letting a lucky shot upset their focus and confidence.
- Clear-minded captains make the right calls; clear-minded keepers and fielders catch with soft hands and throw down stumps; and clear-minded umpires make accurate decisions.

Part B.

INTRODUCING THE GAME MINDSET.

The Most Important Tool.

Mindful Cricket is about one thing that powers a thousand other things: mindset. No one masters this game with the wrong mindset, and everyone can play better with a Game Mindset.

Mindset is the beliefs, thoughts, attitudes and habits you bring to the game and it is the most important tool you have because it can make every other aspect of your game better.

Own Your Space – Hold Your Shape.

Over many years of consulting to Olympic athletes and international business leaders, I've seen and studied the distinctly different mindsets of people who tap their full talent and potential, and those left disappointed and underachieving. Everyone is motivated to do well, but the effective mindset - which I call Game Mindset - is poised and confident, whereas the alternative invariably showcases the four enemies: a reactive mind, distraction, making it complicated and being slow to change.

To see these enemies at play, just watch a batsman struggling with form. They might start with being ultra-defensive, then try the opposite by hitting their way out of trouble, all the while tinkering with grip, stance, back lift and game plans. The batsman is distracted and faces a game which feels overwhelmingly complicated.

We've all been there, and we know different thinking is needed, but we need something reliable and well trained to fall back on so we can learn and adapt fast. We need a Game Mindset. To better understand it, reflect for a moment on how mindset shows in the way a player "owns" the space around them, and in the physical "shape" of their game.

Own Your Space.

In the "moments that matter", a batsman with a Game Mindset will project a sense of balance and calm around them. It will show in their little rituals and sense of order and consistency, which will contrast with the player who isn't in control of their space and looks rushed and disorganised.

Olympic athletes talk about this as creating a small "cocoon" around themselves. This is the small space they control, and it is fundamental to reliable performance under pressure. Cricketers who own their space do it at a pace and in a way suited to them, and it's repeated over and over again.

Hold Your Shape.

Good coaches and observant commentators often note that a player is "losing their shape" or "holding their shape". What they are noticing is mindset projected through physical movements.

A batsman losing their shape is out of balance, perhaps pushing too hard at the ball or getting outside their natural range of strokes; a bowler might be overstriding or falling away in the follow-through; and a keeper could be getting ragged in their footwork and glove work. The opposite is easy to see: players look balanced and fluent because they are holding their shape despite full-on exertion.

A player with a Game Mindset looks in control because they are owning their space and holding their shape. That's Mindful Cricket, and you can unlock its power and simplicity by learning to develop your own Game Mindset.

Game Mindset in a Nutshell.

Here is the mindset of nearly every cricketer who has consistently mastered his or her game in Tests, first-class, club, school or courtyard cricket:

CLEAR MIND Composed, focused, keeping it simple and adapting fast.

PLAY BRAVE Bold vision, putting it on the line, and holding the tension.

PLAY CLEVER Bringing cricket smarts to their game.

PLAY BETTER Applying a growth mindset, game ready and optimistic.

That's it. And you'll see elements of this mindset in batsmen, bowlers, keepers and fielders in every game you watch from now on.

Watch a batsman and you'll be asking yourself from the first ball:

1. Clear Mind, or scrambled?
2. Playing Brave, or too reckless or too tentative?
3. Playing Clever, or misreading the game situation?
4. Playing Better, or struggling to learn and adapt?

Game Mindset - a Stance for the Mind.

You couldn't imagine a batsman without a stance. The stance is the framework onto which everything else is attached. A good stance is balanced, simple and gets the batsman ready to play the ball. There are wide differences in stances from the on-the-move styles of Steve Smith and Joe Root to the poise of Meg Lanning and Rohit Sharma.

Game Mindset is like the batting stance. It's simple, balanced and gets you game ready. It is the key to playing Mindful Cricket.

Game Mindset in Action.

A familiar cricket story helps to highlight the four pillars of Game Mindset because once you learn to recognise the behaviour associated with each element, you'll start to see if your own Game Mindset is limiting your game.

Any book about Game Mindset must include examples of Virat Kholi, and few are better than his innings of 82 in Mohali at the 2016 T20 World Cup:

Needing to win to secure a semi-final spot, the home side, India, were struggling through the loss of three early wickets, and an injury to Yuvraj Singh which curtailed his customary power. Kohli admitted later to struggling to focus because of Yuvraj's troubles, however gradually building momentum in the chase, Kohli partnered with MS Dhoni to calmly push deliveries into gaps and running hard to accumulate the twos that gave them a platform from which Kohli struck seven of nine boundaries in the final five overs. In just twelve deliveries he took India from needing 39 off 18 deliveries to 4 off the final over.

After the game Kohli described the innings as one of his best (ESPNcricinfo Staff 2016), and gave a wonderful insight into his mindset:

MS in the end kept me calm… I could have gotten over-excited. This is what you play cricket for. You need new challenges in every game.

Clear Mind, Play Brave, Play Clever, Play Better: Is there a better example in the modern game than Virat Kohli?

Your Game Mindset is Unique.

You can learn from players like Virat Kohli, but it is also important to realise everyone has their own unique Game Mindset. How do you identify and develop a Game Mindset to suit your own personality and game?
Remember the four enemies:

- Reactive Mind
- Distraction
- Making it Complicated
- Slow to Change.

Did you notice how Kohli kept composure and didn't let his mind get ahead? Those thoughts would have created feelings which could have pressured him to go too hard too early. He kept it simple, adapted quickly and shaped the momentum of the game.

Like Kohli, your mindset needs to avoid those four enemies. You do that in Mindful Cricket by understanding the mindset you currently bring to the game, and then making improvements using the practices, activities and tools covered in the coming Chapters and on the website www.mindfulcricket.com.

> **MINDFUL CRICKET TOOL: Game Mindset Checklist**
>
> *Here's a simple 4-point checklist to use in any game situation to reflect on your current mindset:*
>
> - **Clear Mind** – *composed, focused, and keeping it simple?*
> - **Play Brave** - *looking for ways to succeed (not to avoid failure)?*
> - **Play Clever** - *reading the game and making smart choices?*
> - **Play Better** – *well prepared and open to learn?*

Awareness, Acceptance and Action.

One of my clients is a good club cricketer who'd never made a century, despite reaching the 80s and 90s many times. His story is a good example of how to identify, develop and hone a Game Mindset. Here it is, briefly outlined in the three steps in any personal change process, which you will see employed repeatedly throughout this book:

Awareness: He began by reflecting on past innings using a Game Mindset Checklist. Immediately he realised that his two priority areas for improvement were losing composure and worrying about failing to reach the century, rather than being brave and going for it.

Acceptance: He accepted that it was his mindset causing the problem, and he was responsible and capable of making positive change.

Action: He took action by learning and practising to maintain composure, and by creating and executing a simple plan which focused on his game and not the score. Within two matches he scored the century and went on to score many more and play at First Class level.

Trust Your Game.

Cricket is a game of differing tempos and varying intensities, so when you really understand how to create your own Game Mindset you can relax and trust your technique and talent to produce better results in many different settings. Others will see it unfold in the way you own your space and hold your shape in the moments that matter. You'll know it because it is the mindset you need to be the best cricketer you can be.

Let's get to know the Game Mindset.

CHAPTER 4

The Game Mindset Framework.

This chapter is a high-level run-through of the whole Game Mindset Framework so you can understand the basics and how the four pieces fit together.

The Four Pillars of the Game Mindset Framework.

There are four pillars to Game Mindset:

- Clear Mind
- Play Brave
- Play Clever
- Play Better

Each pillar is developed through core principles and a host of practices, activities, drills and tools.

Here is an overview of each pillar, including what it means and why it's important, and how the core practices will help you to play Mindful Cricket.

Clear Mind.

A Clear Mind is composed and focused in the moment, has simple plans and adapts in an instant. This lays the foundation for all aspects of Game Mindset because clarity is the key to being the best we can be. And creating a clear mind isn't just valuable for your cricket, it is absolutely a life skill which brings benefits to study, career and family life.

A Clear Mind is built on **four core principles:**

1. **Cultivate Composure.** Composure is many things. It's calmness and poise in tense moments, it's patience to deal with frustrations and setbacks, and it's accepting the ups and downs of cricket and life. Mindful Cricket is developing the composure to make better decisions, stay true to your values and goals, and hold your shape in batting and bowling so that rhythm, timing and touch are your strengths while others might lose theirs.

2. **Focus in the Moment.** Minds go to what interests them, which means we're often not giving full attention to the moment. At the heart of mindfulness is the skill to quietly, patiently bring your distracted mind back to the present. Of course, it's natural to want to revisit the dropped catch or poor decision. Mindful Cricket is strengthening the ability to be fully tuned in to what is happening in the present moment, because that's the only place you can make runs or take wickets.

3. **Keep it Simple.** Simplicity is knowing and doing the basics, playing to your strengths and applying pressure to opponents. In the search for an edge we can make it complicated. Mindful Cricket is being aware of the risk of making things complicated, and then going back again and again to three practices: Do the Basics, Play to Your Strengths, Apply Pressure.

4. **Adapt Fast.** This is about developing your ability to play in unpredictable and fast changing situations. It's thinking on your feet and using "learning loops" in the moment (and in your life) to plan, do, check and adapt. Mindful Cricket is crafting a mindset of fast learning and adaptability because that's how to bring your best to the moments that matter.

Play Brave.

Imagine the big wave surfer paddling into a monster swell. As the wave propels them up and forward, there is a split second to commit or withdraw totally. Being too brave or reckless risks serious injury or even death, while being too tentative risks being caught when it's too late to withdraw, resulting in the horrifying plunge into the pit of the wave.

Performance psychologists have found the advantage lies with the bold and decisive person, the one who goes towards the challenge and knows and trusts their abilities.

Play Brave isn't about recklessly swinging at every ball, tossing up inviting leg breaks, or bouncing the best opposition batsman relentlessly. Sometimes it's brave to play with restraint and not bowl your best delivery until the batsman is looking comfortable. It takes courage to defend the good deliveries in a 20/20 game, knowing you'll take responsibility to guide the team home later.

Play Brave is built on **three core principles**:

1. **Create Your Bold Vision**. Bold is choosing what success means for you in the short and long term. Bold cricket is aiming towards your goals, projecting positive body language, seeking small victories and believing good things will happen in even the toughest of circumstances.

2. **Put it on the Line**. Courage is certainly facing Mitchell Starc or batting through the heat of Dubai. However, it is also Joe Root calling out homophobia, it's Suzy Bates speaking openly about mental health and suicide, and it's Steve Smith pouring out his heart asking for forgiveness for letting down his team and country. It's you risking the quick single to give your teammate the strike, it's playing the bold shot, and it's saying what no one else will say at the team meeting because you know it needs to be said. Putting it on the line is the willingness to be vulnerable, to go for what you want and know is right.

3. **Hold the Tension.** This is about persisting when things aren't easy and continuing to apply pressure when results aren't coming. It's resisting the temptation to try for a wicket ball late in an over, or not giving up your wicket with a wild shot because you are struggling to get bat on ball. Cricket matches are so often won by the team that holds the tension.

Play Clever.

Cricket is a game of momentum with an ever-shifting dynamic between bat and ball.

It's not just the "weapons" we bring or the strengths of our opponents that determine success, but how cleverly we deploy those strengths and time our moves to Absorb And Apply Pressure. Clever batsmen work the ball for singles and play in partnerships, while clever bowlers deploy subtle variations built on consistent line and length and read the batsmen's weaknesses.

Play Clever is built on **three core principles**:

1. **Bat Smart.** This is about building trust in your batting basics, like holding your shape under pressure, and learning to adapt to change, building partnerships and applying and absorbing pressure. It's bringing the quality of mindset to match the quality of your technique and talent.

2. **Bowl Smart.** This means learning how to read the game and bringing smart and subtle variations to shift momentum. It's also about knowing your game, working in bowling partnerships and adapting to change.

3. **Keep and Field Smart.** Keepers play a vital role in setting and maintaining standards in the field, and in supporting captains and bowlers to apply pressure. When keepers and fielders bring a Game Mindset, they can make even an average bowling attack look awesome.

Play Better.

A few months after I began working with the Australian Olympic Team, something challenged my mindset about talent and learning. Having grown up playing cricket, I always believed the best cricketers were the most talented because I'd heard experienced Test Players say good players didn't need coaches, and they should just rely on their natural skills.

What changed my mind was observing that the best Olympic athletes were certainly talented, but they were also amongst the hardest working. Psychologists working on the tennis and golf tours confirmed the same observation, which led me to one of the most important concepts in performance psychology: Growth Mindset.

Growth Mindset (and its opposite, Fixed Mindset) was revealed by Stanford University psychologist Carol Dweck (2008) over decades of research on achievement and success. Her findings were simple and compelling:

Our most basic abilities can be developed through dedication and hard work, despite the belief of many that talent is fixed. A growth mindset drives players to get better because they act on the belief they can learn and improve whereas a fixed mindset has the opposite effect.

Play Better is built on **three core principles**:

1. **Apply a Growth Mindset.** Here we explore three growth mindset strategies commonly employed by high performers: taking a strengths-first approach, finding and accepting feedback, and taking care of yourself.

2. **Be Game Ready.** Awareness of what makes you think and feel at your best, and the daily habits to consistently make that happen are the foundation for clever cricket. Then it's about using these insights to create your pre-game and pre-performance routines and rituals.

3. **Bring Optimism.** We see the world differently depending on whether our "mindset filter" is optimistic or pessimistic. Developing your

optimistic filter means learning and applying a way of thinking which reduces anxiety and improves confidence and outcomes.

Approach Cricket Mindfully.

We play our best cricket (or do our best at anything) with a clear and composed mind, fully focused on the challenges of the moment. We don't play so well when our mind is cluttered with thoughts or distracted by unhelpful emotions.

It's likely you are already tempted to go out and begin applying Game Mindset based on what you just read. You can see the four pillars. They look simple, so why not just get on with it?

Players with reactive minds make exactly this mistake. They go into games with the intention to have a Clear Mind and to play bravely and cleverly, and after a few weeks they can't figure out why it's not working as well as they'd hoped. The reason is obvious. They know what the four pillars are, but they haven't made the effort to deeply understand the core principles, and to use the activities and tools to embed them into daily habits and cricket thinking.

Each of the four pillars of Game Mindset has principles you cannot break, or you'll soon end up back in reactive mode.

It will take time and effort to find, develop and hone your Game Mindset and it will be worth it, not just because of the benefits to your cricket, but also because these are life skills you can apply in study, career and other endeavours.

The next Chapter explores the mindset you bring to cricket and seeks to discover the unique triggers to being at your best. From that foundation, the following four sections take you step-by-step through how to create the Game Mindset you need to be the best cricketer you can be.

Key Point Summary.

- Game Mindset is poised and confident, whereas the alternative invariably showcases the four enemies: a reactive mind, distraction, making it complicated and being slow to change.
- To better understand Game Mindset, reflect for a moment on how mindset shows in the way you own the space around you, and in the physical shape of your game.
- Game Mindset is like the batting stance. It's simple, balanced and gets you game ready. It is the key to playing Mindful Cricket.
- When you really understand how to create your own Game Mindset you can relax and trust your technique and talent to produce better results in many different settings.

Mindful Cricket is understanding and accepting the challenges of the game and then learning and applying the principles of mindfulness and performance psychology to develop your own Game Mindset.

CHAPTER 5

Discover Your Unique Game Mindset.

We begin with the central concept in sport psychology: 'the zone'. Here, in a nutshell is the perfect place to understand what Game Mindset means, and to learn what's unique about yours.

No doubt you've heard a cricketer, tennis player or golfer say they were "in the zone"; they had a mindset of total focus and immersion in the game, with little self-consciousness and all the energy, rhythm and confidence flowing in the right way.

Have you had that experience of batting or bowling almost effortlessly? Of bowling with rhythm and natural control of line, length and variation, and of batting with such confidence you see the ball early and clearly, letting it come to you, and striking it easily through the gaps in the field?

Peak Zone and Performance Zone.

A word of caution. There is a mix of scientific research and a few embedded myths about 'the zone' that do little to help most sportspeople. For example, when Olympic athletes talk of 'the zone', they are usually thinking of peak performance, because, as you can imagine, every athlete wants to be "in the zone" on the day of Olympic competition (once every four years doesn't give you much room for error!).

"Peak performance" isn't a particularly useful or accessible concept for most sportspeople because you can't turn it on like a switch when you need it, and it is a small target.

What is useful is to be aware of your mindset when you feel in control of your game. It's not peak performance, but more a "performance zone" in which you play your better cricket. Some players refer to this as their "A-Game", and most seem to experience it around 25-30% of the time.

The mindset associated with A-Game is a great place to explore and discover what triggers or blocks you from playing at your best. It will help you understand what is unique about your Game Mindset, and that will set you up to choose and apply the Mindful Cricket principles and practices in ways that best suit you.

How the Zone Reveals Your Unique Game Mindset.

A cricket match is about to begin. You jog onto the field with your team-mates and then stand back a moment to observe what's happening. Some are running and tossing the ball to sharpen their reflexes, the opening bowlers are pacing their run-ups, and others are stretching and looking at the sky, adjusting their eyes to the surroundings. The opposition openers are approaching the pitch.

Imagine you can see each of your teammates' and opponents' mindsets by the colour of their cap or helmet:

- **Blue Caps** are in the mindset to achieve. They're active, sharp, energetic and confident. They feel in control of their game and are looking forward to getting into the contest. They're ready to take a sharp catch, to bowl with energy and rhythm, or to play each ball on its merits.
- **Red Caps** are in the mindset to attack. They're more hyped or psyched than the blue caps. They might be feeling really nervous, impatient, or even frustrated. They're more likely to be impulsive. You'll see it in bowlers running in faster and being very aggressive, or in the batters playing high risk shots. They might succeed, but the percentages aren't good over the long term.

- **Orange Caps** are in the mindset to avoid. They haven't brought the right energy, which might be because they're tired or bored, or they're preoccupied with fear, doubt and worry. They don't have their usual zip as bowlers, they're slow to respond in the field, and as batters they look tentative.

The caps are "mind zones." Blue Cap, or Blue Zone, is where we play our most consistent cricket. Red and Orange Zones don't mean you won't do well - there's just a lower percentage chance of success.

REFLECTION QUESTIONS

What coloured "mind cap" do you usually wear onto the field?

What makes it change colour?

How much of your cricket success and enjoyment comes down to wearing the right mind cap?

How valuable will it be to learn ways to get that Blue Cap on more often?

Think Blue Zone to Get More Control of Your Game.

The blue zone is the place to really get to know, because it reveals the blueprint for your unique Game Mindset, while reinforcing the value of having a Clear Mind, and Playing Brave, Playing Clever and Playing Better.

Do you notice feeling more in control of your game in the blue zone? It's not trying to control things but rather the timing, rhythm and energy that make you feel near the top of your game. Starting an innings, bowling the final over, or keeping to a spinner on a fast turning deck all seem easier when we think and feel in control of our game.

When players don't feel in control of their game, they make bad choices and underperform. Batsmen misjudge line, length and pace, while bowlers struggle with consistency and rhythm. Wicket-keepers and fielders fumble opportunities and wonder how they could miss something so simple.

The more you feel in control of your game, the better your choices, because you naturally experience the four pillars of Game Mindset. Your mind is clear and composed, your focus is on what matters, and instead of having a cluttered mind with its distractions, pressures and complicated plans, you keep it simple and adapt fast.

Activity: Finding Your Performance Zone.

This activity will help you discover the triggers to your mind zones, and to get better at creating blue zone experiences. It will also lay the foundation of understanding why the core elements and practices in Game Mindset are so effective in developing a mindful approach to your cricket.

. . . .

Instructions:

The activity is designed in four steps, each of which requires self-reflection:

1. Understand your performance zones
2. Capture insights for action
3. How to find your blue zone triggers and blockers
4. Go for Blue

Guidesheets and *Toolsheets* for this activity are available at www.mindfulcricket.com.

STEP 1: Understand Your Performance Zones.

This first step is divided into three mini-activities to explore the three mind zones.

What is Your Blue Zone?

What do you experience when you are in the blue zone? Reflect on these questions about what you *think, feel* and *do*:

- What is your "blue zone thinking" and how does it affect your performance?
- How does being in the blue zone affect the way you feel?
- What do you do better when you are in the blue zone?

Using the blue zone examples as a guide, make a list of how you think and feel, and what you do.

Blue Zone Examples

How I Think...	How I Feel...	What I Do...
Quick and clear decisions	Calm and composed	Rhythm and timing
Clear in mind	Alert	Agile footwork
Simple plans	Confident	Judging line and length
In the moment	Optimistic	Executing plans
Let setbacks go	Energetic	Holding good shape

What is Your Red Zone?

What do you experience when you are in the red zone? Using the examples as a guide, make a list of how you think and feel, and what you do.

Red Zone Examples

How I Think...	How I Feel...	What I Do...
Cluttered mind	Impatient	Overhit the ball
Rushed and Pressured	Edgy and off balance	Bowl faster
Look for the big shot	Frustrated and reactive	Lose shape

What is Your Orange Zone?

What do you experience when you are in the orange zone? Using the examples as a guide, make a list of how you think and feel, and what you do.

Orange Zone Examples

How I Think...	How I Feel...	What I Do...
Distracted	Worried	Tentative shots
What might happen	Full of doubts	Slow to react
Not making a mistake	Lethargic	Passive and defensive

STEP 2: Capture Insights for Action.

Take a few moments to reflect on your notes about the blue, red and orange zones, from Step 1.

Also, recalling the exercise with the different coloured caps, read this brief insight from a player's journal about this activity, to stimulate your thinking:

· ·

PLAYER'S JOURNAL

The blue zone activity helped me recognise how often I've been pushing myself into the red. When I look back on the last few months, I can see I've lost composure and confidence and become more impatient and easily frustrated. That's not my Game Mindset *– so I've got something to work on now which feels simple and about my game.*

· ·

Jot down your insights about the differences between the three zones and how they impact your enjoyment and performance. Reflect on how your blue zone brings with it the Game Mindset pillars of having a Clear Mind, Playing Brave and Clever, and being quick to learn and adapt to Play Better. It is your unique mindset, so get to know it well!

Now we move on to find the triggers and blocks for your blue zone.

STEP 3: How to Find Your Blue Zone Triggers and Blockers.

Triggering your blue zone isn't like the law of gravity - it doesn't always work. However, there are many Mindful Cricket practices which will help to make this more consistent.

Before doing that, it will be valuable to explore why you experience the blue, and to also understand the causes of red and orange, because they are blocking you from more time in the blue.

There are at least six ways to trigger the blue zone. The mini-story below shows how they all connect to cricket.

*A cricketer meets a **challenge,** which fits with their **goals/purpose,** and feels it's achievable at a **stretch.** So, they **clear** their mind, **focus** intently on the challenges at hand, and use the **feedback** on their performance as motivation to learn, adapt and perform. They reflect on their experience and realise these six elements triggered their blue zone.*

Let's unpack these six items briefly.

Find a Challenge:
- What sorts of challenges trigger your blue zone?
- How does your attitude affect this?
- What situations or challenges push you into the other zones?

Set Meaningful Goals:
- What goals or purpose seem to bring out your best?
- When do goals or lack of goals push you into red or orange?

Stretch Yourself:
When you "size" a challenge and feel it's achievable at a stretch, that is usually a great motivator. However, many players under-estimate their abilities and over-estimate the challenge, which doesn't help them to feel in control of their game. Any thoughts?

Clear Your Mind:
- What helps you to bring a Clear Mind to practice and games?
- Are there things in your physical preparation that help?
- Are there thoughts or actions which make you feel less clear and in control?

Focus Intently on the Challenges at Hand:
- How effectively do you stay in the present moment?
- What takes your thinking away from the present moment?
- What helps you to set aside those thoughts about what's happened or might happen, and to refocus on the present moment?

Open up to Feedback:

- What's your mindset towards feedback from coaches and teammates?
- How do mistakes and setbacks seem different when you are in the different zones?

STEP 4: Go for Blue.

Mindful Cricket is continually learning and refining ways to trigger the blue zone. From your initial reflections on the questions above, can you see how this is as much about changing unhelpful practices which push you into red or orange, as it is about doing things to get the blue experience?

A simple way to create a summary of the first steps to create blue zone experiences is to use a Stop–Start–Continue Plan:

Stop or Do Less:	What can you stop or do less to get more time in blue and less in red or orange?
Start or Do More:	What can you start doing or do more to get more time in blue and less in red or orange?
Continue:	What habits, rituals and actions should you keep doing to create blue zone experiences?

This introductory activity builds awareness of your blue zone and lays an initial foundation which you can build on by being mindful of how the way you think, act and feel triggers your mind zones.

The Zone and Mindfulness.

In the context of Mindful Cricket, we are just scratching the surface of "mindfulness", a very popular concept amongst people interested in improving their overall wellbeing and effectiveness. The practices of mindfulness are now regularly incorporated into Olympic and professional sports training, and there is fast growing acceptance in the business world of the value of mindfulness in managing stress and enhancing composure and focus.

The scientific definition of mindfulness is, "the self-regulation of attention with an attitude of curiosity, openness, and acceptance" (Bishop 2004).

Put simply, that means a cricketer applying mindfulness demonstrates two core skills. First, they can bring their focus of attention into the present moment when needed, and second they deal with whatever happens with composure and confidence (because they are open to learn and not trying to change things that are out of their control).

Can you see how the blue zone is a state of mindfulness? In Mindful Cricket, the term "mindfulness" describes the state of mind and way of thinking which can help you to find the blue zone. That state of mind is composed, focused when needed in the present moment, and uncomplicated. The way of thinking includes many of the blue zone triggers, such as accepting things as they are, being patient, open to experiences and learning, and trusting instinct over control.

Mindfulness is a field with a deep history which has been explored and explained by researchers and writers like Jon Kabat Zinn (1994) in Wherever You Go, There You Are and Eckhart Tolle (1997) in The Power of Now. I encourage you to visit www.mindfulcricket.com for references to books and programs which explain in much greater depth this important and potentially life changing subject.

The Cricket Academy.

This is the first in a series of cricket stories and scenarios designed to help you to understand how mindset impacts performance, and how Mindful Cricketers develop their Game Mindset.

The Cricket Academy scenario is set within a team of developing international cricketers who are travelling and learning as they play against strong national and international teams. In the first scenario we join them on a big day, and in the second scenario the players are debriefing their performance to learn more about the zone.

SCENARIO 1: Mindset in Action.

A wicket fell, sending Pradeep scrambling to find his gloves and helmet amongst the jumble of team gear. Rushing onto the field he stole a quick glance towards his family seated in the shade of a giant fig tree, then headed towards the centre for the most important innings of the season.

His mouth was dry, heart pounding and eyes darting around the field as he joined his batting partner Monty on the edge of the wicket square.

"Take a few balls to get set, it's turning and bouncing a bit more than you expect," suggested Monty to his teammate, who was more intent on adjusting a strap on his right pad. Pradeep glanced at the dry pitch and the roughened patches as he arrived at the crease and was greeted with some ungenerous comments from the much older opposition keeper, who laughed as his voice broke slightly when asking for middle and leg guard.

Just under six overs to go and a run rate of seven an over seemed worse with the fall of two quick wickets. How things had changed. Just three overs ago Pradeep had thought victory was all but assured, yet now the momentum had shifted, and the tight circle of infielders clapped and celebrated as he played each of the first three deliveries into what seemed an impenetrable ring.

The bowler, a tall thin off-spinner, spotted the new batsman's frustration when the fourth ball - a slightly short delivery outside off stump - was brilliantly fielded at point, preventing an almost certain boundary. He motioned to his captain and after a brief discussion they brought in the long on for the final ball of the over, leaving an inviting space in the outfield for a batsman feeling the pressure to get off his own duck, and to keep the team's score moving.

Pradeep wondered what his teammates would think if he played out the maiden. Scanning the field, he spotted the gap from mid-wicket around past deep mid-off and hatched a plan. Monty looked at the same space but was thinking something quite different.

Unfortunately, Pradeep didn't notice three things that could have saved him.

First, he didn't notice the bowler deliver the ball from half a metre behind the crease; second, he was unaware how tightly he was gripping the bat with his right hand; and finally, he didn't watch the ball closely enough to see it drop well short of where he expected.

The shot looked awful and the result no better. A half slog, half sweep from two metres down the pitch skied from the top edge straight into the safe hands of the deep mid-wicket fielder.

Instead of guiding his team to a famous victory, Pradeep trudged from the field, tossed his bat angrily towards his bag, and sat sulking for the rest of the game which, despite a brave innings from Monty, fell three runs short.

GRANDSTAND VIEW

What can we learn from Pradeep's experience?

- Was he physically and mentally ready to bat when a wicket fell?
- How could he have reduced the extra pressure he appeared to feel as he headed onto the field?
- What about his focus and body language before facing the first ball?
- How did it appear to others, and what would you suggest he could change, to project more confidence?
- What did you think of Monty's advice, and do you think Pradeep heard it?
- If the bowler could see Pradeep's frustration, did Monty have a role to play in settling him before that last ball of the over?
- What about Pradeep's plan to hit into the mid-on space?
- Was it a reasonable plan? What did he do that made the execution more difficult?

We can never know exactly what was going on in Pradeep's mind. However, we can imagine ourselves in the same situation and reflect on how to give ourselves the best chance of doing well. Let's see what happened next.

SCENARIO 2: Zone Debrief.

It was the first practice session since the disappointing performance.

"Grab your cell phone, or pair up with someone who's got theirs handy," said the performance psych coach, motioning the players to join him in the shade near the edge of the oval, about 50 metres from the nets.

The players sat in pairs watching a short video on their devices about the blue performance zone and the contrasting red and orange zones. As soon as the video finished each player picked up a Find Your Zone Toolsheet. On it was a summary of the messages from the video and instructions on how to explore their blue zone thoughts, feelings and behaviours.

After a few minutes, they shared what they'd written. For many it was the first time they had really thought about how they played so well when their mindset was blue, and how their failures were so often because they'd been thinking and feeling red or orange.

Next the Coach handed out a second Toolsheet called Zone Debriefing, which prompted the players to write examples of thoughts or feelings, and how these affected their behaviours and actions on the ground.

Pradeep's Toolsheet read like this:

How I was thinking and feeling in the red zone:

- *Really nervous at the start of my innings*
- *Felt pressure to keep the score moving*
- *Got distracted by my own thoughts.*

How my red zone changed what I do:

- *Started off tentatively*
- *Took unnecessary risks*
- *Lost control of the shot; lifted my head and tried to overhit it.*

In the final part of the activity, each player wrote a simple plan for what they'd like to do differently next time to trigger their blue zone (or be mindful of playing when in the red or orange).

Pradeep read out his three points to his activity buddy just before they headed to the nets to practise their new skills.

How I will get more blue:

1. *Have all my gear ready when a wicket falls*
2. *Plan with my batting partner – don't just take it on myself*
3. *Be calmer and more confident.*

It was a great start, because the players now understood how their mindset had been affecting their game and could see what to do about it.

GRANDSTAND VIEW

What can you learn from this debriefing activity?

- What insights do you think the players will have gained from reviewing their blue zone experiences?
- If you reflect on a recent game, what would be on your Toolsheet about the impact of the red or orange zone on your behaviour and decisions?
- What three things are key for you to be in your blue zone in your next game?
- How might you build a Zone Debrief into your post-game activities? How often would you do this?
- What value would you hope to get from the debrief?

Debriefing is an important practice because it drives the all-important feedback and learning which is essential to playing better.

Key Point Summary.

- The zone is an ideal place to begin to understand what Game Mindset means and to discover your own unique mindset.
- Core to that mindset is the blue zone in which you feel more in control of your game, and that means a clearer mind, bolder decision making, clever thinking and openness to learn and play better.
- The red and orange zones often create lower performance because thoughts and emotions have the opposite effect to those of the blue zone.
- By being mindful about your thoughts, feelings and behaviours, you can learn to create the conditions for the blue zone – or at least reduce the red and orange.

The next section takes a deep dive into the four pillars of Game Mindset, exploring the foundation principles, tools and activities.

Mindful Cricket is based on mindfulness, which is both a state of mind and a way of thinking. That state of mind is composed, focused in the present moment (when needed), and uncomplicated. This way of thinking is developed through Game Mindset practices.

Part C.

GAME MINDSET – THE FOUR PILLARS.

Establishing the Pillars.

You've probably already realised the four pillars of Game Mindset are not all equal.

The first, Clear Thinking, is the force multiplier for the other three.

Play Brave without Clear Thinking can be risky, reckless or even downright dangerous, such as trying a ramp shot at the wrong time.

Play Clever without Clear Thinking is a contradiction. Cluttered thinking misreads the game and makes poor choices, such as releasing the pressure on a batsman who is on the verge of playing a false stroke.

Play Better without Clear Thinking often means overthinking, overpreparing or getting lost in technique and analysis instead of keeping it simple.

And so, we begin with Clear Mind and explore how to develop composure and focus, and to then capitalise on that foundation by keeping it simple and adapting fast. From there three pillars, Play Brave, Play Clever and Play Better each offer three core principles to add to your game as needed.

My recommendation is to put priority on composure and focus because they are indeed the force multiplier, however amongst the other pillars are a wide range of practices, activities and tools to help you create the mindset you need to be the best cricketer you can be.

Game Mindset.

Play Brave

Clear Mind

Play Clever

Play Better

Pillar 1.
Clear Mind

Finding Clarity.

We know a Clear Mind is the centrepiece of Game Mindset, but how do you create that clarity when it's needed?

Well, you've already started by identifying and understanding your natural Game Mindset (Blue Zone), so here are three questions to ponder a little further as we work through this Section:

- What triggers a Clear Mind for you?
- What gets in the way and creates cluttered thinking?
- How does that affect your enjoyment and performance?

The insights you gain, and the practices you learn and adopt in this Section will have benefits well beyond cricket, because a Clear Mind makes work, study and life easier and more enjoyable.

What's the Opposite of Clear Thinking?

A Test player with a reputation for mental toughness and composure wrote this in his journal and shared it with me during a coaching session:

PLAYER'S JOURNAL

I've learned that everyone goes through times in their careers where it's harder to concentrate and keep things in perspective. It's happening right now. However, when I was younger it would really worry me, so I'd just try harder, which had the opposite effect by just adding to the pressure.

Now I know I play best with a clear mind, and that means being mindful and slowing it down a bit to put less pressure on myself. Instead of overthinking I keep it simple, and I'm also working on taking the weight off myself by being more realistic about the short-term successes or failures.

I'm good enough to play at this level, I just need to trust myself to learn and adapt in the moment.

What a brilliant example of the four core components of a Clear Mind: Composure, Focus, Simplicity and Adaptability!

We all experience it at times. It's perfectly normal. The cluttered mind, the racing feeling of stress or pressure, the self-imposed expectations and distractions, giving too much attention to things we can't control, and over-thinking what should be a simple game. That's not just a cricket challenge, that's a life challenge.

Choose a Simpler Pathway.

We want to be our best, enjoy the game and achieve success, but somewhere in amongst the expectations and pressures we lose focus on what matters and make it harder to succeed. Frustration builds, confidence drops, and we make complicated plans for what is essentially a simple game.

You can quieten the noise, reduce the clutter and take the weight off yourself. It starts with awareness of the blue zone, and this section features practices, activities and tools to make that happen more often. Each is a Mindful Practice designed to help you to be in the moment and to strengthen your ability to choose how you want to respond rather than reacting emotionally.

This pathway to help you feel more in control of your game covers four core principles, each of which contributes to a Clear Mind:

- Cultivate Composure
- Focus in the Moment
- Keep it Simple
- Adapt Fast.

These principles are laid out over the next four Chapters, and the order in which they are introduced is important.

Think of this like a chess game where the two most important pieces are the King and Queen. Composure is the King and Focus in the Moment is the Queen. These two are foundation mindfulness principles and practices which take on the enemies of reactive mind and distraction.

To quote Jon Kabat-Zinn (1994), a leading thinker and practitioner in mindfulness and author of *Wherever You Go There You Are*:

> *Mindfulness practice means that we commit fully in each moment to be present;...with the intention to embody as best we can an orientation of calmness, mindfulness and equanimity right here, right now.*

With those foundations in place we move to action by Keeping it Simple, to reduce complication and speed up our ability to learn and adapt.

TOOL EXAMPLE: Clear Mind Debriefing.

To set the scene, here's a super-simple example of a Mindful Cricket tool used by a leading international player after each innings to help develop a clearer mind (each question was rated on a 1-10 scale):

1. Was I composed?
2. Was I totally focused on what mattered?
3. Did I keep it simple?
4. Did I learn and adapt quickly?

The debrief of this tool revealed that when the score was 8 or above on the four questions, the player consistently reported "I felt in control of my game" and performed better and therefore enjoyed their cricket as a consequence.

Let's do the same for you!

CHAPTER 6

Cultivate Composure.

Composure is not the absence of emotion. Don't for a moment assume composed players aren't feeling anxious, angry, frustrated or deflated. More likely they've trained themselves to project positive body language while letting those natural but uncomfortable feelings roll through with no more attention than they deserve.

When a batsman walks to the middle and takes guard, they can be both composed and nervous. How? By accepting and welcoming the uncomfortable feelings instead of avoiding or fighting against them.

Emotions are powerful. Anger, impatience, fear, joy, shame, frustration, and disappointment all compel us to do something - to be reckless, to be tentative, to be aggressive, to be bold, and so on.

Mindful Cricket is building three lines of defence to the bad choices and the disappointing outcomes which come from lack of composure that uncomfortable feelings can generate.

That's why we have emotions. The good news is that we can choose how to respond to our own emotions, and to a great extent we can learn to give them less power.

Of course, it takes courage and strength to stay calm and poised when feeling anxious and fearful, but there's enormous power in realising all significant growth and development comes from feeling uncomfortable. Read those words again and say them to yourself: all significant growth and development comes from feeling uncomfortable.

Let's explore a little more about composure and then set up those three lines of defence.

Cricket Composure.

Composure is many things: it's the calmness and courage to hold your shape against the fastest bowler you've ever faced; it's the patience to stick with your plan when your mind wants to give it up; and it's accepting the poor umpiring decision and getting on with the next delivery.

Composure is invaluable in the heat of competition because it helps you make better decisions, set the example for teammates, and even intimidate opponents. Think of the best tennis players, golfers, footballers and cricketers. Composure in moments that matter wins more championships than talent and technical skills combined.

Here's an excerpt from the journal of a very good cricketer who shares his personal experience of losing composure and how mindfulness improved the situation:

PLAYER'S JOURNAL

Learning to stay composed is one of the best things I've ever done. From my earliest days as a cricketer I'd get super nervous starting my innings, and I struggled to stay patient when a bowler had me pinned down. As a bowler I could lose it with a poor umpiring decision or a dropped catch. It was when I was introduced to Cultivate Composure that things started to change. I learned to be much less critical of myself and to use the breathing and calming rituals to stay focused in the moment.

It's easy to recognise the heroes and villains in this story.

Meet Two Villains.

Let's start with the two "big" villains, which are called The Inner Critic and The Noisy Mind.

1. The Inner Critic

Early in our cricket careers we learn to grip the bat, get our head in line with the ball, catch with soft hands and move through the crease when bowling. However, with few exceptions, we never learn how to quieten the inner critic who points out our limitations and mistakes, constantly compares us to others, makes situations seem overwhelming, and creates all manner of fears and worries, most of which never happen.

Have you met this critic? To build composure, we need to quieten our inner critic and instead learn to deal with someone more reasonable and positive.

This theme of quietening the inner critic is one we will revisit many times because it is such a common cause of loss of self-belief, focus and performance.

2. **The Noisy Mind**

Day-to-day life is hectic. Instead of entering a cricket game composed and focused, players are over-hyped and distracted by their own thoughts or what's going on around them.

Think about it. Does your day-to-day life train your mind to focus calmly and intently on one thing and to do it well, or does it encourage you to be constantly thinking of something in the past or speculating about the future?

No wonder people feel their mind is full of noise and static!

Enter the Heroes.

Fortunately, where there are villains there are often heroes.

Imagine the pilot of a passenger aircraft fighting to control their stricken plane. It's not just technical know-how that will give them the greatest chance of survival, but rather the composure to use their know-how to make the best choices. Their heart will be pounding, stomach churning and muscles tightening as the natural fear response kicks in. Flashing thoughts of potential catastrophe, of their families and what might have been had they flown a different plane all flood into consciousness.

The pilot I want is well trained and brings three Mindful Practices which act as lines of defence against loss of composure. First, they accept the uncomfortable feelings of fear in their body and are not alarmed by them. Second, they tap into an inner calmness which has been practised (mindfully) for these moments. And third, they deflect their own inner critics' thoughts of catastrophe and instead focus on solving the most essential problems.

My pilot's mindset helps to slow down, to quieten the noise and to take things one at a time - sound familiar for cricket? They use their skills and knowledge, while others experience an ever-faster, more out-of-control situation.

You are probably not an airline pilot, but you do have these mindset skills ready to be developed:

1. **Awareness and acceptance of uncomfortable feelings;**
2. **Your inbuilt ability to find calmness or stillness despite what is happening around you;** and
3. **A rational, logical mind.**

Let's explore these three lines of defence against losing composure.

MINDFUL PRACTICE 1: Accept Your Emotions.

You are the product of millions of years of evolution.

Your very existence proves your ancestors had a Game Mindset which kept them safe from all sorts of threats to their survival. They didn't face fast bowlers, or drop catches in front of packed grandstands, but they did face the real possibility of tigers or hostile tribes hiding in the forest and attacking at any moment.

They felt the same queasiness in their stomachs, the same pounding heart, and the same edginess and doubt you feel going out to bat, or when the game is on the line. While that discomfort might hinder your cricket game, it was the difference between life and death for them.

Your ancestors survived because anxiety and fear motivated them to avoid risks or be ready to fight and win if needed. And they did this every day for thousands and thousands of years, while evolution eliminated those who got it wrong.

That means you have inherited a finely tuned radar which loves to pick up and exaggerate threats. It is very helpful for surviving tigers, but in a modern world the tigers are mostly in our minds, so we end up anxious, frustrated or angry when we'd rather be excited, composed and ready to play.

Seven Signs Your Body is Telling You It's Getting Ready:

- Faster breathing
- Pounding heart
- Dry mouth
- Queasy stomach
- Tense muscles
- Need to urinate
- Dizziness.

These are reflexes. They are valuable, short-lived, and (with a sensible inner critic) they are all signs that you are good to go.

· ·

PLAYER'S JOURNAL

I never realised nervousness could help me play better. That feeling in my stomach used to make me lose confidence and feel weaker, but now I tell myself it's just my body getting ready for battle. I actually look forward to those feelings now because I know it's sharpening my mind and getting me in the blue zone.

· ·

It's a reflex. You can't just tell yourself to be composed when your mind thinks there's a tiger coming. No way!

- **Your body** gets ready for fight or flight. You feel the surge of adrenaline, the queasy stomach, the pounding heart. It feels like life or death!
- **Your mind** sees danger and decides what to do. Chances are the inner critic is running the show, and its tigers are fear of failure and over-blown expectations.

- **You take action** by taking flight or readying for a fight. Neither of those is about composure, which means we need a different mindset to play Mindful Cricket!

Mindful Cricket is cultivating an attitude of expecting and accepting the "fight and flight" feelings. It's practising the stillness techniques we're about to cover and building them into daily and pre-game rituals. Then you are in much better shape to find that blue zone.

That mindset starts by accepting that uncomfortable feelings are okay, and in fact they're extremely helpful, provided you don't interpret the feeling of adrenaline and extra blood pumping through your body as anything other than a natural response designed to get you game ready.

REFLECTION QUESTIONS

What pre-game nerves or other uncomfortable feelings do you experience?

Do they affect your confidence and focus, or are you able to accept them and let them be?

What about the important moments in a game?

What's your awareness of helpful or unhelpful feelings?

Is there an opportunity to step back and remember those ancestors who helped you to be wired for competition?

Can you learn to accept and embrace the uncomfortable feelings?

Moods and Emotion.

An important point here is the difference between temporary emotions and moods. The latter last for a longer period of time. If these moods are concerning you – for example, being anxious or depressed - then it's time to chat about it with your doctor or a counsellor or coach, because they'll be able to help you understand what's happening and how best to handle those concerns. One thing we do know about evolutionary emotions is that feelings help us to understand each other better; so, it's not only perfectly natural to talk about emotions, it's an important way to break patterns of thinking which can be unhelpful if we keep them to ourselves.

MINDFUL PRACTICE 2: Find Your Calm Centre.

This practice is about learning to find the stillness or "calm centre" within your mind and body and bringing attention back into the present moment. This is amongst the most powerful of mindful practices to enhance well-being and performance, because it reduces the power of those uncomfortable feelings.

We begin with the basics, showing you activities to apply personally and within a team setting.

At www.mindfulcricket.com you will find more information on this practice, called *Centring*, together with more advanced mindful activities and tools, including resources and specific training schedules.

To provide a very practical guide to these basic first steps, here is my story of introducing this practice to a Club Team in a State League in Australia.

SCENARIO: Introducing Mindful Stillness and Calm to a Club Team.

The First Session as a Group

The players gathered in the room adjacent to the changing area under the small grandstand, they were changed and ready for a meeting and the practice session to follow.

In the days leading up to the meeting, their coach had handed out a short summary of Game Mindset for them to read, and he asked players to leave phone devices in lockers. They were expecting a 30-minute session and listened intently as the coach shared some stories and praise for mindfulness skills.

With the scene set he introduced me for what could be a make-or-break session, because despite the obvious value of mindset in cricket it is still a topic some players dismiss without giving it go.

ACTIVITY 1: Clear Your Mind – Begin With Stillness.

To reassure the players that this would be practical and valuable, I opened with a quick summary of what was to come: "Don't expect anything remarkable to happen in the first session or two," I explained, "Just observe and we'll see what you notice."

And so we began with a set of guided instructions. "Settle into a comfortable, well balanced position on your chair with your feet flat on the floor, and hands in lap. Choose whether you'd prefer to keep your eyes open and gaze at a spot ahead of you or to close them."

When the players had mostly stopped their shuffling, I continued. "For this next five minutes I'm going to ask you to do nothing more than sit relaxed and still, and just observe what that feels like, including how thoughts come and go in your mind. To take away the distraction of how much time has elapsed, I will set a timer to lightly chime once per minute."

I sat quietly, observing the players and coach as they experienced this simple but challenging first step on a journey that promised great rewards for those willing to persevere.

"What did you notice?" I asked of the players after the fifth chime. A few were laughing uncomfortably while others were taking a moment to adjust to the light.

"Nothing," observed one of the fast bowlers, with a laugh.

"Nothing?" I queried, and then paused, waiting for someone to fill the quietness.

Soon players were adding their thoughts: "I noticed how quickly my mind was thinking about other things"; "I noticed my breathing"; "I noticed my back aching", and then a final comment from the fast bowler, "I noticed it's hard to sit still."

"Excellent." I nodded, congratulating them on successfully completing the first training exercise for their mind. Most looked unconvinced until I added, "Is there any chance your mind just did exactly what it does in matches?" A few players got it. "Does it go where it wants to go?" More players nodded. "That's why this training is so important, because you've got the opportunity to train it to go where you want it to go."

Stillness is such a simple yet powerful practice, which directly contributes to having a Clear Mind. Just reflect for a moment on what athletes like Formula One drivers do just before competition. Most will be quietening their minds. They know the adrenaline will kick in and get them up when the race is about to begin, so they sit quietly and find that stillness inside themselves.

Of course, in day-to-day life it takes self-discipline to pause and just be still when there are so many distractions like social media to grab our attention. The value to be gained is enormous, so read on now about Centred Breathing, and then decide if you are willing to build a short ritual of stillness and Centred Breathing into your life.

The use of breathing or the breath as a trigger for calmness and focus is a foundation for many advanced mindful practices. It seems almost too simple, so before I continue with the story, here is a brief Player's Journal Report which describes the benefits of the practice:

· ·

PLAYER'S JOURNAL

Breathing is the key to my mental game because it's so natural and gives me three real advantages. As a daily ritual it calms me down so I'm less reactive than I used to be in sport and work. In games I use it to bring back composure, and it's also part of my set up every delivery. Every cricketer should do a mindful breathing course, the benefits are excellent.

· ·

ACTIVITY 2: Centred Breathing for Composure (10 minutes).

The second activity in the opening session was a ten-minute Centred Breathing activity based on a script which is available at www.mindfulcricket.com, and which I also encouraged the players to practice at home. These are a few of the key guide points:

- Take your seated stance again with feet flat on the floor, hands in your lap and begin relaxing as you draw the breath into your belly.
- Bring the breath in while keeping your shoulders and chest relaxed and still, noticing your belly rising and falling with each inhalation and exhalation.
- Explore the effect of the breath. What happens if you take a slightly deeper breath and then exhale while letting go of any tension in your body and face?
- Pause for a comfortable few moments after exhaling. There is a silent space there, a calmness you might discover with practice, which many athletes use as a focal point for their mindful relaxation.

Most of the players were genuinely immersed in the rhythm of their breath and the feeling of inhaling, pausing, exhaling and pausing. I reminded them to connect the experience of stillness in the first activity with the rhythm and sense of relaxation from focusing on the breath. With practice many people come to recognise a stillness or calmness within themselves, to which their own breathing rhythm and pace is the entry point.

During the second half of the session I asked the players to be aware of their thoughts.

"Pay attention to the breath and be mindful when your mind wanders, as it inevitably will, and just patiently return your attention to the breath. Accept whatever you feel now as being what is now. Avoid judging yourself. Just focus and breathe, and when you realise your mind has drifted, bring it carefully back to the breath."

Many would have been confident they didn't need that advice. However, after a few minutes with quiet reminders to focus on their breath, I called time, allowing the players to re-orient themselves in the room before sharing their experience.

"I'm not very good at this!" exclaimed one player, shaking his head and breaking the silence.

"Why do you say that?" inquired their coach.

"Because I couldn't stay focused on my breathing for more than a few moments."

"Were you able to bring your attention back to your breathing?' I asked.

"Yeah," said the player cautiously.

"How many times?"

"Maybe half a dozen," said the player, laughing at noisy agreement from most of the room.

I reassured the players there can't be such a thing as bad centring practice, because either you stay in the moment, or you spend your time bringing your thoughts back. If it's the latter, then it's much like doing repetitions in the weight room or throw downs in the nets. Weights build body strength, and centring builds mind strength.

The key to Centred Breathing is to do it, without judgement. Some sessions will be more relaxing and focused than others, but the key is perseverance, because the value comes from the consistent application.

I handed out Centring Guides with personal practice activities and online links for foundation training in Centred Breathing and encouraged players to find ten minutes each day to practise the activity.

Over the next two weeks we ran three more group Centred Breathing sessions, and each time asked the players if they'd been able to find the time for their practice sessions. Just over half the team bought into the approach. It was a great start.

Centred Breathing - A Few Pointers.

It's not particularly useful or interesting in a book to write out detailed scripts for centring and other mindfulness relaxation and meditation activities. Accordingly, I intend to use www.mindfulcricket.com to provide free and subscribed resources for you to use personally or with your team. Here are a few pointers for now:

Lighten your expectations: In the first few sessions of centring, it's very common for people to be negative and self-critical when their minds wander a lot. The wandering mind is perfectly natural; a key to mindfulness is to stop the self-criticism (leave that inner critic behind) and be more accepting of what is. A good mindful breathing session is one you do irrespective of what happens. For most players it takes a few sessions for them to accept this fact, and when centring becomes a daily habit the vast majority notice differences in composure and focus. Many also report better sleep.

Train to strengthen the core: Developing your centring skills and practices is like strengthening your "mental core." Just ten minutes a day to calm your mind and body, and gently direct your attention back into the moment, will pay big dividends. Breath is incredibly powerful because all your emotions have a distinct breathing pattern, and it's something you can access at any time.

Find the quiet space: When practising the breathing techniques, imagine the space between your breaths as the quiet centre. I find this quiet space most easily after I exhale. However, if I'm feeling stressed or anxious, then the space between inhale and exhale is better because I use it to get the effect of the release of tension with the breath. Experiment with both to see what works best for you.

Experiment: Download a few free apps and have a try at a mix of guided meditations (where someone is guiding you). All practice is valuable and the more you get used to observing your breath and patiently guiding your attention back into the present, the more resilient these skills will be when you are in pressure situations.

Visualisation/Mental Rehearsal. One of the key tools of sport psychologists is visualisation (also known as imagery and mental rehearsal). I see this as a natural extension of the mindfulness activities discussed in this section, so give thought to how you can weave mental rehearsal into your practice. It can be a valuable tool in preparing for matches, and also an adjunct to skills practice.

The majority of my clients across sport and business have a daily practice of some form of mindfulness relaxation and meditation, which helps them stay calm and composed in high stress situations.

As Tim Gallwey, author of *The Inner Game of Tennis (1979)*, noted:

When the mind is fastened to the rhythm of breathing, it tends to become absorbed and calm. Whether on or off the court I know of no better way to begin to deal with anxiety than to place the mind on one's breathing process.

If Cultivating Composure is important to you then this is a great ritual to make part of your life.

MINDFUL PRACTICE 3: Quieten the Inner Critic.

We all have an inner critic who can devastate even the best attempts at cultivating composure.

Does your critic ever say any of the following things:

- I'm never going to take wickets on this pitch
- I'm hopeless at playing the short ball
- I hope I don't drop a catch
- I can't believe I dropped that catch. I am such a bad fielder
- If we lose another wicket, I can feel a collapse coming.

Notice the characteristics of the inner critic: All-or-nothing thinking, rehearsing mistakes, and focusing on weaknesses. Of course, the critic works like pouring petrol on those uncomfortable emotions like nervousness, anxiety, and worry. It's no wonder we lose composure!

Mindful Cricket cultivates composure by helping you to be more aware of how self-limiting thoughts drive feelings, and what you can do to take back control. Make sense?

Great. Let's do it.

SCENARIO: A Personal Story.

Why do we have an inner critic? Can these negative thoughts have value? Surely they are a sign of weakness in our mind?

I was fortunate to be studying psychology early in my representative cricket career and asked my professor exactly these questions. His answer made a big difference to my sport and professional career.

In brief, what he said was:

Everyone has this inner critic and it's trying to protect you. It developed when you were a kid because important people like parents and teachers criticised you and pointed out mistakes and dangers. They did it to keep you safe from harm like hot surfaces, nasty people and embarrassment, which made complete sense when you were a kid. However, as you grew up you became more competent and independent, but some of those early beliefs stayed and they became your "inner critic".

For example, I don't want my 3-year old son crossing the road because he can't make safe decisions, so I tell him it's not safe. Basically, I scare him by telling him about danger and how he can't handle it. That triggers uncomfortable feelings like fear, which is good. However, the sooner I coach him to have the belief in his ability to navigate roads, the better.

Of course, if my son never learns to replace those early fears with belief in himself then he'll likely have an irrational fear about crossing roads as an adult. The critic will fire up those uncomfortable feelings and he'll go miles out of his way to avoid difficult intersections.

I found it very helpful to realise my inner critic was just self-protection. I could understand how worries about being smashed all over the park, not keeping up with the fitness training, or getting nailed by a fast bowler were my critic's attempts at avoiding embarrassment. But I wanted to play First Class cricket, and that meant facing failure and fast bowling head on; so, it was time to get a hold of that inner critic and replace him with something my professor called an inner coach.

The coach showed me how my own thinking was holding me back, and challenged me to lean into the uncomfortable emotions, instead of giving them so much power. It worked very well, so here's how you can do exactly what I did to quieten the inner critic.

ACTIVITY: Quietening Your Inner Critic.

This mindful activity shows how to quieten and replace your inner critic with an inner coach to cultivate self-belief and composure.

· ·

Instruction:
Follow the three-step personal change process of Awareness, Acceptance and Action:

1. Awareness of how the critic limits your thinking
2. Acceptance that it's your thinking stirring up uncomfortable emotions
3. Action to coach yourself to be mindful and composed.

This tool is available at www.mindfulcricket.com.

STEP 1: Awareness - Meet Your Critic.

Start with the *Toolsheet,* or write out the statements below which describe three of the most common beliefs which motivate an inner critic:

- I want to avoid **mistakes** because they are embarrassing
- I want to avoid **losing** because I want to prove I am good at cricket
- I want to be **liked** and **approved** of because I am part of a team or club.

Now take five minutes to recall times when thoughts about mistakes, about losing or being approved of stirred up uncomfortable feelings or held you back in some way. Record the feelings and the situation.

Here are some examples a young cricketer recently produced in an individual coaching session:

> **Mistakes:** *Frustrated at training when playing poor shots. Tentative bowling my opening over. Embarrassed when dropped catch last Saturday.*
>
> **Losing:** *Annoyed when dismissed. Angry when we lost the match.*
>
> **Approval:** *Anxious didn't want to speak up at team meeting.*

The point in creating this list is to step back and be aware of the connection between your thoughts, your feelings and how you act. For example, the young cricketer mentioned above had an inner critic who was intolerant of mistakes. That was causing him to avoid taking risks or making mistakes. It was holding him back.

He used the table below to reflect on the extent to which the beliefs of the inner critic and inner coach applied to him. He could clearly see that his mindset was about avoiding mistakes. Can you see any that apply to you?

	What My Inner Critic Believes	What My Inner Coach Believes
Mistakes	It's embarrassing making mistakes. I should avoid putting myself in that situation. Mistakes show I'm not good enough.	Mistakes are part of learning. Get comfortable with being uncomfortable. Mistakes are the pathway to get better.
Losing	I'm only a good cricketer when I'm in form. Winning proves I'm good. It's important to be better than others.	I'm a good cricketer. Form and winning come and go. My aim is to be the best I can be.
Approval	People won't like me if I'm different. Don't try my newest delivery in matches. Follow what others are doing.	People aren't thinking about me. I have some unique strengths. Trying new things is important.

The statements in each column show it's not hard to imagine how a bit of game pressure fires up the critic and upsets composure by turning attention towards weaknesses and difficulties.

The good news is you are now mindful of how your thinking affects the way you behave, which means you can choose to do something about it if you want to.

STEP 2: Acceptance - It's Your Critic in Action.

The next step is a classic mindfulness exercise. Just be aware of when your inner critic shows up during the week and in the next match or two.

Use the *Toolsheet* or your Journal to note when the inner critic shows up, how long it lasts, and what happens. For example, you might notice you are thinking about what could go wrong before going out to bat, or at times in the field you could be hoping the ball won't come to you.

It's your choice now to lean into the uncomfortable feelings and remain composed in the way you think and move. For example, frustration about mistakes doesn't have to be acted on. You can choose to let the feelings roll through because it's unlikely they'll last for more than 30-90 seconds at the most.

Remember the Centred Breathing exercise, when you just observed your feelings without judging them? That's training you to let feelings roll over instead of driving you to action.

STEP 3: Action - Give Your Inner Coach Equal Time.

The final step is to use real-life situations to actively quieten your critic by pausing and talking through the situation using an inner coach voice. For example, if you beat the bat twice with perfect outswingers and then get hit for four and get really agitated with yourself and the batsman, the critic is around!

The solution can be simple:

- Take a breath and pause.
- Observe the critic and the self-defeating thoughts without judgement.
- Ask this coaching question, *What's the basic thing to do here?*

Try it now. Imagine you are bowling, and the inner critic is stirring up uncomfortable feelings. Take a breath and pause, observe the critic, then relax your grip on the ball and rehearse feeling the rhythm that will get the ball in the right areas.

Use this simple approach and you might be amazed at how often you've been letting the critic run the show and how easy it is to quieten that down, and coach yourself to be more effective.

Key Point Summary.

- Mindful Cricket is cultivating composure because it helps to find the blue zone in which we make better decisions and play to our potential.
- Our inner critic and noisy mind work against composure. However, we can build three lines of defence: accept our emotions, find centred calmness, and replace the critic with the coach.
- Uncomfortable feelings are okay, and in fact they can be a welcome sign that you are game ready. However, if negative moods persist, it's time to chat with your doctor, counsellor or coach.
- Stillness is at the core of a Clear Mind. Create time and space for stillness instead of just reacting to everything that's happening around you.
- Centred Breathing is the core practice and gateway to composure. Just ten minutes a day can transform your life. Make it a ritual.
- We all have an inner critic and it stirs up emotions with limiting thoughts past their use-by-date. Watch them, let the feelings roll through, and be your own inner coach: take a breath, observe, and then go back to basics.
- Cultivating Composure is not the absence of emotion but being mindful. You don't have to react to every emotion, and it's owning your space and holding your shape when feeling uncomfortable.

CHAPTER 7

Focus In The Moment.

The core question in the search for a Clear Mind was: How do I find calmness and stillness?

If you have settled into any kind of practice rhythm for Centred Breathing, you will be very aware how fickle the attention is and how your mind wanders even when you want it to remain settled. Minds go to what interests them most (driven by feelings), and there is plenty to interest a cricketer's mind.

What if I get hit for another boundary? thinks the bowler walking back to their mark. I'll be taken off and not get another chance. Distracted, they amble in, serve up an inviting full toss and watch helplessly as the batsman drives hard and straight to the boundary.

Two boundaries to my half century, thinks the over-confident batsman just before hitting a waist-high catch back to the bowler.

And so it goes on, a noisy mind driven by feelings, forever thinking about and judging what happened, or wondering what might happen, instead of accepting and dealing with what's happening right now.

To play Mindful Cricket, we need a Clear Mind, which leads to our second core question: How do I learn the art of focusing in the moment? Much of what we have covered about the inner critic and uncomfortable emotions also helps to answer this question. In this chapter we spend a good deal of time in the nets, getting the essence of what true concentration means when batting, bowling, fielding and keeping.

Make Curiosity Your Guide.

True concentration cannot be forced, yet coaches instruct players to concentrate harder without giving them any advice about helpful ways to actually do it. Telling someone to concentrate is like telling someone to score runs. Great idea - but how?

I suggest starting by taking a fresh look at the game of cricket, because you already have the ability to focus in the present moment with calmness and clarity. That's your blue performance zone, but it's not going to happen by forcing it. We need something natural and repeatable.

Bear with me for a moment and closely read this example from a completely different field to see how we can get so familiar with a solution that we miss the obvious.

SCENARIO: Bring A Fresh Curiosity.

Some time ago, I was walking in the city alongside the river and paused for a few minutes. By chance, I chose a spot near an artist perched on a small stool in the middle of a busy pathway, her canvas on a fragile wire stand and a generous array of coloured pencils and brushes in a tray on her lap.

She was a craftsman oblivious to the never-ending swarm of people brushing past or stopping to briefly check her work. She wasn't looking at the scene as if someone had told her to concentrate, she was absorbed with curiosity. And so, the canvas revealed tiny but important details of the river and buildings that I'd missed, despite walking this path most days for over two years. She wasn't just looking, she was observing and understanding the detail in the detail, and as she painted you could see the essence of her craft wasn't pens and brushes. It was touch and feel.

I asked myself, "Are there lessons about focus and attention to detail that we can learn from the artist? Questions that might challenge, and answers that could fundamentally change how we play cricket?"

For example, I wondered if I had ever really looked at a cricket ball when batting. Of course, I looked at the ball, but had I ever seen it as a craftsman would see it?

Had I ever really watched the ball in its flight, seeing and judging the exact swing and position? Or as a bowler had I ever sensed the subtle difference between late or early swing as the ball left my hand? If I was so bad at observing my own city, what had I missed on the cricket field?

How would I bat or bowl if I focused like the artist?

Then it dawned on me.

The art of the great batsman is to see the ball earlier. The art of the great bowler is subtle variation. The art of the wicket-keeper is to set and reset their concentration ball by ball, hour on hour. They don't concentrate harder; they focus all their senses on their craft in the moment.

The answer to my question seems obvious. If I was to bat or bowl with the focus of an artist, it would mean:

- Really watching the ball with curiosity *(***Ball Focus)**
- Mastering rhythm, timing and touch (**Touch and Feel**)
- Switching focus on and off as needed (**Resetting**).

Often, I'm asked by cricketers for tips or tricks to improve their concentration. The answer lies in these three "obvious secrets", but not in the way most expect unless they've had the pleasure of reading Tim Gallwey's classic *Inner Game of Ten*nis (1979), which was so far ahead of its time as a book and way of thinking. As Gallwey advised: *Fighting the mind does not work. What works best is learning to focus it.*

SELF-ASSESSMENT: Focus in the Moment.

Would you like to see the ball earlier, bowl with subtle variation, and reset your focus time and again across the longest of batting or bowling innings? If the answer is *yes,* then take a quick stocktake below to assess your strengths and potential areas for development of your Game Mindset in the key practices of Focus in the Moment.

Instruction:

Reflect on the statements one at a time, then consider to what extent each is true for you most of the time. Those areas where it is not true are areas to apply the Game Mindset practices, activities, drills and tools.

	BATTING	BOWLING	FIELDING/KEEPING
Ball Focus	I really focus on the ball and take it one delivery at a time.	I plan and execute my bowling plans one ball at a time.	I am fully focused and positive as the bowler delivers the ball.
Feel Focus	I have a comfortable stance, and good feel and timing for shots.	I can make changes in my rhythm and hand to create subtle variation.	I move with rhythm and catch with soft hands.
Reset Focus	I can reset my focus after playing a poor shot or losing concentration.	I can set aside distracting thoughts and refocus on my bowling rhythm.	I switch my focus on when needed.

We now explore how to strengthen these three core practices through activities including a range of net drills to do by yourself and with teammates.

MINDFUL PRACTICE 1: Be Curious About the Ball.

Cricketers and coaches have talked about watching the ball since the game began, and yet do you really know how to watch the ball? Do you practise watching the ball, or is your attention on technique and scoring runs, and the ball just happens to be a part of the process?

Advice to watch the ball isn't enough to create Mindful Cricketers, so we go back to basics, to restart your relationship with a cricket ball, and to use your own natural curiosity and attention to break through to a new level of focus in the moment.

The following activities build on each other and include net drills together with brief accounts from players of their experience with this approach. As mentioned earlier, many of these are inspired by the initial work of Tim Gallwey.

ACTIVITY 1: Discover the Detail of the Ball.

This activity brings you back to the most basic of cricket skills, watching the ball. It is intended to build awareness of what that actually means.

- -

Instructions:

Find a cricket ball and open your mind to seeing and doing things that might at first seem too simple and obvious. Persevere. They have remained hidden to most cricketers for over a century, so it's easy to dismiss the obvious when we don't see it.

Imagine you are the artist, your object is the ball, and the aim is to get a crystal clear, detailed mental picture of the ball.

Place it where you can observe it from many angles, but don't touch. Take a few Centred Breaths to calm your mind, and then set your attitude to be as curious as a child seeing a cricket ball for the first time. Avoid judging the activity, just do it for 3-5 minutes.

What do you see?

What colour is the ball? What changes in shading do you observe across its parts?

What is that thing around the middle of the ball? A seam? Can you observe more than five things about the seam? Colour, material, consistency, thickness, threading…?

How is the surface of the ball? Rough, smooth, shiny? Is it four pieces or two?

Is it round? Any dents or imperfections? Anything else you can see?

- -

When you've studied the ball, sit back, take three Centred Breaths and consider the Reflection Questions about how you watch the ball when batting.

REFLECTION QUESTIONS

Do you really seek out the ball and lock onto it like a sharp spotlight?

Do you look for the seam?

Do you study its spin or swing?

Do you watch it with relaxed concentration, or are you more strained and tense?

Have you ever thought about what "watch the ball" actually means?

Do you sense the possibility of improvement from going back to the most basic instruction in cricket – "watch the ball"?

After completing the reflection choose a time for the next activity, in which you will practise your concentration using the ball as the object in a net session.

ACTIVITY 2: Spot the Seam.

This activity taps into your natural skills of concentration and focus as you look for the seam of the ball. With practice it can help you to relax and see the ball and its pathway more easily.

Instructions:

To practise your ball focus, allocate 5-10 minutes in a batting net with a medium pace bowler or someone doing throw downs.

Take your stance, use your usual forward or back press, and instead of just watching the ball or thinking about your shot, put all your attention on how early and sharply you can see the seam of the ball after it's delivered.

Don't be concerned about playing good shots or being dismissed. Clear your mind, be composed, and your natural senses will play the shot. Just aim to bring "active calmness".

It might feel strange to be so relaxed, or to be looking for a part of the ball. Initially you might feel you won't be ready; however, your mind is like a well-functioning computer, so if you feed it the right information it will make the right decision.

Your coach is always there to help with the technique when it's needed.

Here are some examples recorded in player's journals, of their experiences using this incredibly simple approach to improving their focus.

PLAYER'S JOURNALS

Eddie (Club Cricketer): *I tried the curious mind approach to batting, and it was amazing what happened. For the first five minutes of every practice session I really focused on looking for the seam. It took a few sessions to do it and be calm and alert, but I soon realised how badly I'd been focusing before, so I just made it my normal practice. I then added the thought to let the ball come to me, which meant I was playing as late as possible. Pretty soon I was picking up the line and swing really early. It's helped me to be much more relaxed and balanced early in my innings, and I'm letting balls go I would normally have poked at.*

Smriti (Club Cricketer): *I had a real problem playing leg spin and I'd been trying all sorts of changes in my technique which weren't working, so I used the curious mind idea. My coach got me to say, "Where's the spin?" as the bowler delivered the ball. She set up two full net sessions where I just worked on staying relaxed, looking at the angle of the seam as it was spinning and not worrying too much about the outcome of the shot. By the time we finished my feet were moving again and it was like my mind just knew when to go to the pitch of the ball and when to play back from the crease.*

Ishat (International Cricketer): *I used it against fast bowlers because I wanted to get better at judging line and length. I realised I hadn't been focusing on the ball, but more on my thoughts about what sort of delivery it was going to be. It was making me tentative, so I've been working in the nets on using the Centred Breathing to be calm and ready, and then I've tried to spot whether the* *seam is straight or scrambled. Our quicks offered to start off at medium pace and to get me used to the pace, and it didn't take long to be still and clear in mind. I'm just so much more balanced and focused now.*

· ·

When first doing this activity, the two biggest challenges are to put aside your initial need to not be dismissed or to strain looking towards the ball. As you'll see from these journal stories, the players "retrained" themselves to observe the ball in a more relaxed and curious way. It took a few sessions, but they all found this helped to create a Clear Mind, and their natural ability took over.

MINDFUL PRACTICE 2:
Tune in to Touch, Feel and Rhythm.

Touch, feel and rhythm is the ball leaving your hand, it's your body position, timing, and even the sound and feel of the ball hitting the bat.

Think for a moment about what cricketers take for granted. How a bowler adjusts their point of release by millimetres to change the length of delivery by half a metre; or how they impart the spin, the pace and the trajectory they'd imagined fleetingly at the top of their mark. And how the batsman deftly dabs a late cut or drives a ball on the up through the covers without thumping a clumsy chest-high catch to the fielder.

These are the skills of a craftsman and make you realise it is close to a miracle of coordination when you just toss the ball accurately back to the bowler!

To keep this as simple as possible, we go to a player's account of their experience using Touch and Feel Drills to improve their focus on the present moment.

SCENARIO: Touch, Feel and Rhythm Drills.

*I've always found it easier to bowl with pace and rhythm in the nets than in match-
es. My coach suggested it was about my focus, so we worked on some "Touch, Feel
and Rhythm" drills.*

Over a month I practised four drills and the result has been great.

*The first drill was to bowl into a net off a couple of paces with my eyes closed.
That helped get a sense of the rhythm and release feel.*

*The second drill was doing a series of slow-motion run-throughs of my action,
and from that we picked a couple of areas to refine.*

*The third drill was a competition set up by my coach at each practice session.
It was a six-ball competition where the batters were teeing off like it was the final
over of a 20/20. My task was to bowl the six balls with rhythm and pace into set
target areas on the pitch.*

*The final drill was the coach standing a couple of metres from the stumps and
calling the line and length to bowl as I ran past. This drill was brilliant because it
really trained me to hold my shape while bowling under pressure.*

*I'm much more confident now in backing my own action in match situations
instead of being mechanical like I was before.*

ACTIVITY 1: Getting to Know the Ball.

To develop to a new level of focusing, we need to not just see the ball, but
also know how it feels in our hands and on the bat, so this exercise is
intended to raise awareness before you get into the net drills.

. . . .

Instructions:
Again, use your Centred Breathing as a mini-ritual at the start of
the activity (it's good practice for what's to come) and then take 3-5
minutes or longer if you want, and be slow and curious. There's no hurry.

Pick up the ball. How does it feel? Heavy or light? Big or small? Rough or smooth?

What is the feel in your fingers, in your palm, and how is that felt in other parts of your body?

Notice that everything is involved.

How do the different parts of the ball feel?

Put yourself in the role of different styles of bowlers: quicks, spinners and seamers; left and right hand.

What do you notice when applying different grips?

Toss the ball and catch it. What is the feel as it leaves your hand? How does it spin? What happens to the seam?

Which part of your hand or hands does it land in? Can you feel the seam as it lands in your hand?

Toss it again, although this time imagine the seam is fragile and might break if it hits a hard surface.

What changed in the feel of the catch? Did you "give" more with your hands?

Throw the ball as high as is safe and count the number of times it spins. How many times did it spin?

Can you double the number of spins and catch to protect the seam?

Do you see the darker and lighter sides of the ball as it spins?

What happened?

And then realise you've been like the artist. Absorbed in the detail, just focused and working with the ball.

· ·

Can you see how the secret switch to concentration lies in giving your mind challenges and approaching them with curiosity?

ACTIVITY 2: Sound and Feel.

This incredibly simple drill can have a huge effect on batting focus and confidence, by taking the mind off technical details and tapping into natural rhythm and timing.

. . . .

Instruction:
Pick up a bat and ask someone to do a few throwdowns in the net.

Instead of thinking of technique or shots, focus only on the sound and feel of the ball hitting the bat. That sound and feel will vary but you'll know when it's in the sweet spot.

. . . .

Most players find it best to initially do this drill with throwdowns, but pretty soon they're ready to take it into full-scale net practice. I've had many players say it's a great way to break out of bad form patches, because putting attention on the sound and feel of the ball and bat seems to get their timing right.

ACTIVITY 3: Bowling Rhythm Awareness.

In the latter stages of limited overs matches when quick bowlers struggle to land a yorker and spinners lose control of length, the loss of focus can be caused by all manner of things (nerves, fear of failure, poor planning, etc), but ultimately it comes back to being able to bowl with rhythm and control in tight situations. Crucially, we need to do it without being self-conscious or mechanical, and that's where touch, feel and rhythm practice drills come in handy.

. . . .

Instruction:

This two-part activity is based on the practices used by top level golfers and archers, who are highly skilled at forming a plan in their mind and then executing it with rhythm and timing on every shot:

- Eyes Closed Bowling
- Slow Motion Bowling.

PART 1: Eyes Closed Bowling

Pick up a ball and find the side of a net where you can bowl the ball safely without any risk to you or others. Close your eyes and bowl the ball into the net off one step.

Repeat this a few times, being particularly mindful of observing where and how you feel the rhythm in your delivery.

Which parts of your body are involved?

What triggers the movement?

Which muscles flow together?

What's different between deliveries that have rhythm and those that don't?

Pay attention to your legs, hips, chest, shoulders, arms and wrists – all the while just getting to know the feel of the delivery and where power, and perhaps accuracy, comes from.

If safe, continue and add an extra step or two into the delivery and bowl a few more.

This type of eyes-closed exercise is regularly practised by Olympic archers who will think nothing of spending half an hour in eyes-closed practice to get in touch with the feeling of releasing the arrow. Basketballers do the same for free throws. Why don't bowlers do it more often in cricket?

PART 2: Slow Motion

Pair up with a teammate and take it in turns to do slow motion run-throughs of the final steps and release of your action.

Check in with each other by asking what your teammate feels in their action.

What are the key segments?

What seems to trigger each segment?

For example, a medium pacer might notice it feels like they have three "pieces" to their action: the first is coiling like the fisherman beginning their cast, the second is moving through the crease, and the third the flick of the ball leaving the middle finger.

Mindful bowling is knowing and trusting two or three simple cues which help you to create the rhythm or feel you want.

My three cues for outswing were: (1) bounce and energy in the run-up; (2) sight the spot to aim; and (3) zip down the back of the ball. Under pressure, those three were my total focus.

· ·

The feel of your delivery is where to focus – not the scoreboard, not what just happened, or what might happen. Mindful bowling is about rhythm and feel in the moment. All else will look after itself.

ACTIVITY 4: Hold Your Shape.

This drill is one of a series in Mindful Cricket designed to challenge bowlers to retain their shape when faced with challenges from the game. The drill simulates those challenges by creating a late change in plan.

· ·

Instruction:

Mark out your usual run-up and have a teammate stand about 2-3 metres from the bowler's stumps. Agree a set of six target areas: three outside off (short, length and full), and three at middle and off. Number them.

As you pass your teammate and approach the stumps, they tell you a number to hit the required length or line.

Your practice challenge is to deliver the ball with rhythm and energy to the target they've just given you. It's fun and a very good test of whether you can keep your body cues consistent, which means holding your shape.

Here are two other examples recorded in player's journals of their experiences using the style of drill covered in this chapter to improve their bowling focus.

· ·

PLAYER'S JOURNALS

Kirstie (Under 19 National Cricketer – Swing Bowler): *I've been working with my coach on rhythm drills for the past month and it's really helping my focus and rhythm in matches. We always do some eyes-closed work at the start of practice to get into the feel of the release, and then we do game sense practice in competition with the batsmen. I've bowled the final over in our last two matches, and it's been so much easier to hold my shape and rhythm where I used to get tense and try to place the ball.*

Hershelle (Club Cricketer – Off-Spinner): *I never really thought that focusing on my rhythm was important for concentration, but it's been really good. At every practice session I do some drills with the other spinners to reinforce our cues and shape for rhythm. We can see what each other is doing and we can help out. For example, my best action is when I rotate high over the top, and my teammates remind me in games and I'm definitely bowling more accurately and with more bounce.*

· ·

MINDFUL PRACTICE 3: Reset Your Focus.

Cricket, like archery, baseball and golf, is a "stop-start" sport, meaning that players focus intensely for short periods, then drop the intensity, and then focus again.

In my career I've had the privilege of working with multiple World and Olympic champions in both archery and shooting, and early on I learned from them that focus is about the rhythm of switching on – switching off – switching on, and so on.

The outer limit of intense human concentration is somewhere between forty-five and sixty minutes, so it's impossible for a cricketer to maintain high intensity during a full innings. This means it's essential to learn and practise switching concentration on and off, so it doesn't fade when needed most. That's why resetting is one of the key practices to strengthening your Game Mindset skills.

ACTIVITY: 1-2-3 Reset Your Concentration.

Whether you are batting, bowling, fielding or keeping, there's a simple ritual you can use to switch on concentration. It is about owning your space. It builds perfectly from the work on breathing, ball focus and touch and feel.

All the top performers have little rituals that trigger the on-and-off switch. Making it a ritual embeds a rhythm or cadence, which builds consistency and reliability under pressure.

A video of the 1-2-3 Reset method is available at www.mindfulcricket.com.

Instruction:

Pick up a cricket bat and then imagine you are standing near the crease, holding the bat, and you want to reset your focus for the next delivery. It's as easy as 1-2-3 Reset:

1. Look down and step slightly away. Take a slow, deep breath, exhale firmly while rolling your shoulders and loosening your arms. Pause for just a moment.

2. Grip the bat, taking care like a golfer to place it comfortably and securely in both hands. Let your gaze shift from hands to the horizon as you think about readying for the next delivery.

3. Move at your pace into your stance, tap the bat twice and quietly, but firmly under your breath say: "Where's the ball?" as you watch the bowler approach.

Some style of 1-2-3 Reset is used by most top athletes as the foundation for their match day concentration. I observed Cheteshwar Pujara use a similar approach to reset his mind, ball after ball, when his three centuries in four Tests helped India win their first series in Australia.

Think for a few moments of situations where you might find a 1-2-3 Reset useful - for example, at the start of an innings, for each delivery when batting or bowling, fielding in slips, and after a dropped catch. Use your net session to experiment with different batting and bowling resets. Base them on using the Centred Breathing and sigh to release tension, a "physical cue" to Reset your mind, and a short phrase or word to call to action.

There may also be times away from cricket when you want to bring your focus into the present moment, such as listening to a lecture, beginning a presentation or when presented with a frustrating problem. Use 1-2-3 Reset for these.

Examples of Resetting.

One of the most obvious examples of the use of reset in sport is the professional tennis player. Watch a game and you'll see player after player use 1-2-3 Reset: breathing and loosening, flicking the strings of their racquet, and then moving into their serve or receiving position. That's a great example of owning your space.

The call to action I've most often heard from leading batsmen is *Where's the ball?* Off-spin bowlers use cues like *Up and Over* to remind themselves to get energy and height into the delivery, while medium pacers think and even imagine the feeling of *Rhythm and Zip*.

Key Point Summary.

- Minds go to what interests them, so we can benefit from learning how to focus in the moment.
- True concentration cannot be forced.
- You already have the ability to focus in the moment. It's a natural part of the blue zone, so it's not a question of finding a new Game Mindset but tapping into what you already have.
- Curiosity sits at the heart of concentration, and in cricket there are three things to get really curious about: the ball; mastering rhythm, timing and touch; and resetting focus when it's needed.
- Bring a fresh curiosity by really watching the ball and practising a calm attention to the seam when batting.
- Improve your touch, feel and rhythm by mindful activities like listening for the sound of the ball striking the bat, and bowling with eyes closed.
- Make 1-2-3 Reset a ritual you can rely on in any situation.

Like every other aspect of the game, these focusing-in-the-moment skills require practice and are best woven into your habits and rituals, so they work reliably when the pressure is on.

Above all, they are intended to keep it simple, and that's the topic of the next chapter.

CHAPTER 8

Keep It Simple.

Keep it Simple is the third core principle to creating a Clear Mind, and there is no better way to start than with reference (D'Anello 2019) to a quote from Usman Khawaja about MS Dhoni:

He concentrates on the controllables, doesn't worry about the rest, doesn't let a lot faze him, understands there's a lot of ups and downs in cricket.

Australian Test Captain Tim Paine observed in the same article:

What I do love about watching him (Dhoni) play, whether he is batting or keeping and captaining, he keeps things very simple.

Simple is Powerful.

It is not easy to Keep It Simple when feeling pressure, and yet a complicated mind just seems to make things move faster and cause problems to loom larger.

Mindful Cricket is bringing simplicity to what can seem complicated.

Remember the differences between blue and red zone thinking? One characteristic that comes up time and again is simple clarity versus complicated confusion.

Are there players you see in international cricket who seem to have the same ability as MS Dhoni, to think their way clearly through difficult situations? Perhaps a bowler who holds their nerve when bowling at the death in a 20/20, or a batsman who regularly guides their team out of trouble?

You've already got some ideas on how to do that by deploying the Clear Mind practices.

Composure *fosters patience, because things are so much simpler when you play the right shot at the right time or deliver the right ball for the conditions.*

Focusing in the moment *makes things simpler, whereas letting your attention drift to what happened in the past or what might happen in the future makes it complicated.*

Simplicity is powerful, although it's not necessarily easy. However, strengthening your centring skills and bringing focus into the moment offers a brilliant foundation on which to build the clarity that is so connected with runs, wickets and enjoyment of the game.

Simple or Complicated?

We should take a moment to further consider whether cricket is a complicated game full of confusing laws, different formats, changing conditions and endless subtleties in the battle between bat and ball, or a simple game which can be described in one sentence.

As discussed earlier, it's probably either depending on your mindset. Here is an attempt to explain your cricketing roles in one sentence:

When bowling, aim your best stock delivery to consistently hit the top of off-stump; when batting always watch the ball closely and play straight early in your innings; when keeping and fielding, be alert, relaxed with soft hands, and ready to move.

SCENARIO: When It Gets Too Complicated.

I was discussing this concept of "simplicity" recently with an English County cricketer (let's call him Jeremy) who has had success in the T20 leagues as a spin bowling allrounder. He'd lost form and was struggling to handle the pressures. His diagnosis: "I'm making it too complicated".

I asked him to write his thoughts in a Mindful Cricket Journal, because this is a good way to help players clarify what's going on and to be accountable for making the improvement. His comments highlighted those annoying enemies: reactive mind, distractions, and making it complicated.

. . . .

JEREMY'S JOURNAL

My mind is jumbled and racing out on the ground. I'm thinking about so many things it's impossible to be calm and focused. I'm worrying about bowling to batsmen with big powerful bats on tiny grounds. The noisy crowds and comments from the opposition are bothering me more than normal. I'm also feeling the pressure of a one-year contract. Instead of bowling four tight overs, I'm reacting too much, and the past two innings I've had to go for it from the first ball and holed out both times with pretty ordinary shots.

. . . .

My immediate response on reading this was: "That's a lot to take in!"

He laughed and said: "But it's true."

"Is it?" I asked, challenging him.

He repeated the same story. "Bats more powerful, crowds noisier, one-year contract and tight matches."

"Yes, that part's true," I agreed. "However, what role do you want to play in this, because from the sound of it you've given yourself the role of victim?"

He paused and reflected on that. It shook him up a little. He didn't think of himself as a victim. He was a professional cricketer with a good track record.

We talked for a few minutes while I reassured him that he'd simply drifted away from a mindful approach to a reactive approach, and that was making things a lot more complicated than they needed to be.

Keep it Simple With a Go-To-Plan.

Jeremy had spoken with professional footballers about mindfulness meditation and was very interested in the idea of Game Mindset practices and tools to bring that way of thinking into his game. In a Game Mindset Self-Assessment, he acknowledged that a Clear Mind was not a current strength for him, and rated himself low on Composure, Focus in the Moment, and Simplicity.

Two Foundation Practices.

We started with twice-daily Centred Breathing practice sessions, to build the foundation for stillness and calmness that was missing in his game and general life. I expected he'd benefit quickly by quietening his mind because he wasn't normally this reactive.

Alongside that, we set out to rebuild what I call his Performance Rituals, because a video of a recent match showed that instead of looking poised and owning his space through well-paced and consistent routines, he was very inconsistent and looked jumpy and out of control. The starting ritual was the 1-2-3 Reset for both batting and bowling. The aim was for these to become the "mind stance" he would use in tight game situations, to feel more in control of his game and to own his space with suitable pace and rhythm.

With the Centred Breathing and 1-2-3 Reset established, I was keen to help him build a simpler game plan. He'd clearly drifted away from doing the basics and had lost confidence in his strengths and become over concerned with weaknesses and other things he couldn't control. In addition, he certainly wasn't being clever in how he applied pressure on the field. It was time for Jeremy to create his Go-To-Plans.

The Go-To-Plan: What and Why.

A Go-To-Plan is a simple plan built on three mindful practices: back to basics, play to your strengths, and apply pressure to opponents.

The plan helps with composure by taking player's minds off things they can't control (like big bats, opposition comments, and match situation), and instead focusing in the moment on what they can do something about.

Commitment to basics and playing to your strengths makes it simpler, which increases the chances of success by playing the percentages; while the focus on applying pressure gets you out of your own head.

The power of a Go-To-Plan lies less in the content of the plan and more in the confidence and focus from having one to fall back on when things are tight.

Put yourself in Jeremy's position as we work through the three Mindful Practices to create a Go-To-Plan for batting.

MINDFUL PRACTICE 1: Back to Basics.

The essence of a Go-To-Plan is to go back to the basics of the game, because it's less often the heroic shot or delivery that wins the big moments than it is the basics done well and repeated.

Jeremy is batting in the middle order in a short form game. Let's assume it's a mixed bowling attack with spinners and quicks, and the pitch is good for batting. What would you do in his situation?

GRANDSTAND VIEW

What are the basics in this situation if you are in Jeremy's position?

- *How do you prepare to be fully ready when the wicket falls?*
- *What is your routine before facing the first delivery?*
- *What's your basic plan for the first few deliveries?*
- *Is there anything to be ready for when running between wickets?*
- *What's the plan if you get away quickly?*
- *What's the plan if you struggle to score from the first six deliveries?*

Jeremy knew the basics. He realised he'd lost sight of those basics and was making it too complicated, so he identified just a few to really focus on: 1-2-3 Reset for every delivery, head still, short backlift, and playing with intent on all shots.

Here are some examples of basics for the four key activities in cricket, which might be handy when developing your own Go-To-Plan.

Bowling Basics: Stick to the process of disciplined line and length and build pressure in the knowledge that wickets will come.

Batting Basics: Get set for every ball, play within your strengths and build pressure by clever shot selection and good running between wickets.

Wicket-Keeping Basics: Commit to good footwork, watch the ball the whole way into your gloves and trust your soft hand catching technique. Apply pressure by keeping all the fielders working as a team.

Fielding Basics: Understand what's needed in your fielding position, anticipate and watch the ball come to you, apply pressure by cutting off runs and being neat and organised in throwing and ground fielding.

MINDFUL PRACTICE 2: Play to Your Strengths.

The second part of a Go-To-Plan is to capitalise on strengths, because in any game situation the ideal thing to do is to leverage your strengths.

When I first spoke with Jeremy, he was thinking about anything but his own strengths. He was worrying about things he had little or no control over, and then not doing the basics that had got him to be selected in the first place. Why was he trying to hit big boundaries from the first ball? It had nothing to do with ability and everything to do with a jumbled and reactive mind.

It was obvious Jeremy had plenty of strengths: a sound defence; a good range of shots, particularly the onside; he's quick between the wickets; and he's getting stronger in his Game Mindset practices.

BASICS SELF-ASSESSMENT.

I handed Jeremy a pen and a *My Strengths Toolsheet* and asked him to list the bowling and batting strengths he brings to the game. In just a few minutes he had listed many items and was looking and sounding a lot more confident. Here are some examples:

My Strengths

What I Bring to Bowling	What I Bring to Batting
Spin both ways	Sound defence
Can read a batsman	Enough power to hit over the ring
Accurate	Range of shots
Experience and success in different conditions	Experience and success in different conditions
Subtle variation of pace	Quick between wickets

GRANDSTAND VIEW

What are your thoughts about being in Jeremy's position?

- *How can you leverage his sound defence and a good range of shots?*
- *He's quick between the wickets, so how might this help?*
- *How would you plan to use his hitting skills?*
- *He's practised the 1-2-3 Reset. How and when to use it?*

When the mind gets complicated, it is easy to lose sight of our strengths and become overwhelmed by the challenges and our own weaknesses. That's why being mindful is so helpful - a couple of breaths, a reminder of strengths and soon things look so much better.

MINDFUL PRACTICE 3:
Apply Pressure to Opponents.

The final practice in a Go-To-Plan is applying pressure to opponents. This has the double benefit of getting you out of your own head, and also doing things which can shift momentum.

Jeremy is primarily playing short form cricket, so let's begin with an important question: What creates pressure in a short form game? The number one answer is losing wickets, followed closely by maiden overs, or dot balls in the final few overs.

GRANDSTAND VIEW

Climb into the grandstand and give some thought to how Jeremy can apply pressure.

- *He's arrived at the crease well prepared, with a Clear Mind and simple Go-to-Plan. Where can he start exerting pressure?*
- *What body language could he show? Does he look like he's owning his space?*
- *How about clever ball placement and speed between wickets?*
- *Will you back his game judgement and power to hit the right ball into the right spaces?*

Applying Pressure was very important for Jeremy because it got him "out of his own head" and helped him become much more positive and proactive.

Honing Your Go-To-Plan.

Jeremy's Go-To-Plan and the two foundation Mindful Practices (Centred Breathing and 1-2-3 Reset) helped him to quickly forget the lapse in form and settle back into enjoying cricket by playing his game and not worrying about things beyond his control.

Like Jeremy, you can benefit from clear and consistent Go-To-Plans for the key parts of your game. These will create a great foundation from which you can adapt slightly to different conditions, as you'll learn in the next Chapter.

ACTIVITY: The Go-To-Plans for Moments that Matter.

This activity guides you to create a Go-to-Plan for practice and sets the foundation for using the same approach in matches.

Instruction:

A Go-To-Plan is built on three components: Back to Basics, Play to Your Strengths, and Apply Pressure to opponents. Before your next practice session, create Go-To-Plans for batting and bowling, and put them on a card so you have a quick reference point during the session.

Be mindful that a Go-To-Plan should be brief, which means one to three points for each activity (eg line and length, subtle variation, restrict the run rate). The intent is to keep it simple and build your focus and confidence, so less is better.

Batting Practice Go-To-Plan: Take a few moments to reflect on the practices which make up the plan (basics, strengths and pressure), and then answer the questions below:

1. What basics are important? (e.g. early into position, short back-lift, head still and watch the ball)
2. What strengths can you bring? (e.g. solid defence, quick to judge length)
3. How do you apply pressure to them? (e.g. start with positive body language, clip anything on leg).

Bowling Practice Go-To-Plan: Create your bowling plan using the same process as for batting. For example, you might want to work on your "death" bowling in a short form game.

1. What basics are important? (e.g. bowl to one part of the field, maintain rhythm)
2. What strengths can you bring? (e.g. slower ball, accuracy)
3. How do you apply pressure? (e.g. first two deliveries yorkers outside off, follow a blocked run with slower ball because batter is likely frustrated).

Key Point Summary.

- Keeping it simple isn't easy, but the practices of Cultivating Composure and Focusing in the Moment lay a great foundation.
- "Simple" begins with a mindset of focusing on the basics, playing to your strengths and applying pressure.
- Mindful Cricket is attending to what you can control and guiding your mind away from the uncontrollable.
- Do a stocktake of the strengths you bring to the game. It's easy to take them for granted.
- Define the game basics and go back to them to start creating your Go-to-Plan.
- Play to your strengths (and read more about this in *Play Clever*).
- Apply pressure to your opponents through projecting confidence in your body language and using your strengths and the basics.
- Mindful Cricketers don't try to control everything. However, they do take time to set and hone their Go-To-Plans, which means that when it's not working, or confidence starts to waver there is something tried and tested to fall back on.
- The Go-To-Plan is a simple approach seen in the mindset and behaviours of cricketers who own their space and hold their shape when others are losing theirs.

CHAPTER 9

Adapt Fast.

In the 2019 World Cup Semi-Final, in front of a parochial Old Trafford crowd, the favourites India poured the pressure onto a New Zealand team, who made the finals despite relying almost solely on Kane Williamson to make defendable scores. Midway through the New Zealand innings and struggling to get much past four runs an over on a two-paced track, commentators on radio, TV and social media were calling for Ross Taylor to hit out, while Williamson continued to grind away.

History now tells us Taylor top scored and the unexpected happened in so many ways, as it does in cricket. Rain intervened to turn a one-day game into two days, with New Zealand continuing their innings on the second day. India collapsed to be 24 for 4, and then a brilliant 77 by Ravindra Jadeja got them within striking distance, only to be denied by a direct throw from Martin Guptil which ran out MS Dhoni and left India to ponder a massive lost opportunity.

Both teams were in strong winning and losing positions, and both were written off by observers. Of course, one team came out on top, but in their approach to the game, both illustrated why mental agility and adaptability is so important in cricket.

This was a World Cup where scores over 300 had become the norm, so it wasn't surprising to hear people call out for New Zealand to score faster. Williamson and Taylor defied that view, which they would have known was the talk of the grandstand and showed real confidence and adaptability by trusting in their strategy of keeping wickets in hand and fighting through to the end. They displayed all the pillars of Game Mindset: Clear Mind, Play Brave, Play Clever and Play Better.

Both teams showed enormous ability to keep a Clear Mind, so they learned and adapted in a fast-changing environment. They were able to say to themselves: "I can learn to do anything I put my mind to, and I can do it in moments that matter." In sport that's a great advantage, and of course it's a wonderful life skill.

We saw it at play in New Zealand's "all in" commitment to their game plan, in the way they backed their strengths, worked in partnerships and learned quickly from experience. Williamson and his team believed they could find a way to perform and win in those conditions. Others might easily have tried to thrash their way to 300 and been dismissed for a low score which India would have chased down in no time. And is it any surprise that the man of the match, Matt Henry, credited the great bowling effort to a team strategy of applying pressure constantly?

Dhoni and Jadeja showed adaptability as they set short-term goals, took calculated risks, worked together as a partnership, learned from experience and set the next small goals. The commentators could speculate about the end result; the players were in the moment, applying adaptive thinking to navigate through the game moment by moment, goal by goal, and learning as they went.

A World Cup Semi-Final is certainly an unpredictable environment, and so are most games of cricket. Adaptability is essential to playing Mindful Cricket.

Adapt to Change.

What do these situations have in common?
- The batsman can't pick the direction of spin
- Rain interrupts play and shortens the game
- The swing bowler continually beats the bat but is not getting an edge
- A team gets away to an unexpectedly fast start
- Pitch is two-paced.

Of course, there are many answers. However, every one of those situations requires players to adapt or adjust to change. The ball, the pitch, weather, players and the game itself all bring difference, and we need to learn and adapt so success isn't restricted to when conditions are favourable.

SCENARIO.

Observe a top batsman when they're not picking the spin. Can you see them adjusting their game, searching for ways to survive and get on top? Every ball is a mini experiment: batting on off stump to take LBW out of the picture or using their feet to get to the pitch of the ball, maybe getting back or coming down the pitch to hit the bowler off their length or sweeping anything on the stumps.

A swing bowler continually beating the bat without getting an edge needs a similar mindset. Create a plan, do it, check what worked and what didn't, then adapt. Shift the length up a half a metre, go slightly wider on the crease to cut down the sharpness of swing, or maybe decide to persist because the batsman is getting agitated. If that doesn't work, drop in a short ball to push the batsman onto the back foot and then attack the stumps. Be mindful, be patient, use subtle variation.

These examples, and thousands of others, highlight how cricket is a game of adapting, of constantly thinking on your feet. Yet have you ever been trained in how to learn and adapt quickly? Does traditional cricket practice really help to speed up adaptability, or does it have the opposite effect of slowing down the learning process?

You Are Not Alone.

In the business world, terms like "Agile" and "Adaptive Ways of Working" refer to methodologies which transform work situations from slow, process-heavy activities to small, fast, accountable teams who deliver value quickly by planning, doing, checking and adapting in short cycles called "sprints." The mindset behind this approach (which is very similar to the training methods used in many Olympic sports) is rather simple:

To survive and thrive in a changeable environment, we prioritise fast plan-ning, doing, checking and adapting over traditional management and planning approaches.

Being agile in business is about delivering value to customers by adapting fast; and it does that by putting the responsibility and ownership on teams to create cycles or loops of planning, doing, checking and adapting. It works brilliantly because it's nimble and it engages everyone in learning and adapting.

Does it sound like an interesting idea for cricket teams? Small, fast, accountable teams running their own practice sessions; responsible for goals and outcomes; planning, doing, checking and adapting multiple times during the session; measuring and constantly improving. Wow! That might shake up a few traditionalists!

Cricket needs players to adapt fast. Are you willing to give it a try? Are you keen to get better at thinking on your feet? If your answer is *yes*, use the following activities to give it an initial try in the nets, and then consider making it a way of life by taking an hour to get set up and then ten minutes a day to learn and practise a different way of thinking and problem solving.

This process takes a bit of discipline, but there are so many benefits for cricket and other parts of your life that I strongly encourage you to give it a go. Visit www.mindfulcricket.com for more details on this approach.

MINDFUL PRACTICE 1:
Think in Learning Loops (PDCA).

Let's go back to the batsman and the hard-to-pick spinner. The batsman is constantly planning, doing, checking what's working and then adapting. Can you see the thinking-on-your feet "learning loop" that's happening in the batsman's mind?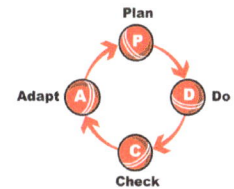

Plan – Do – Check – Adapt.

P: Create the plan. D: Do it. C: Check what worked and was learned. A: Adapt. Then PDCA again, and again and again, with a Clear Mind and a nice balance of Play Brave and Play Clever. One ball at a time, simple and effective. That's Mindful Cricket.

Operating Rhythm.

PDCA (Plan-Do-Check-Adapt) is a derivation of the continuous improvement method popularised by Edwards Deming, an American engineer and pioneer of the Quality Management field.

It is underpinned by a mindset of planning by "looping and learning", instead of the conventional "linear" approach. For example, most cricket teams devise a structured game plan before going out on the field; and the coach plans the net practice session and then players bat and bowl, as they've done for over a century.

The problem with conventional planning is things change, and traditional cricket practice methods fail to equip players with the mindset and tools to adapt fast.

A PDCA mindset solves this problem because teams and coaches agree a brief plan at the start and then create an operating rhythm of learning loops to adjust as things unfold.

For example, when I coach PDCA net sessions, the players are allocated into small teams. Each team is responsible for their own training and development, with the coaches as a resource. The players decide on the goals (Plan), run drills and simulations for sets of six deliveries (Do), build in quick reviews/feedback after sets of overs (Check), and then capture learnings and go again (Adapt). We use a visual board or mini-whiteboards so players can record and update what they are focusing on.

Players really enjoy this approach to practice because it builds in an operating rhythm of PDCA which accelerates the learning process. The benefits include:

1. Greater engagement, because players own their learning and development;

2. Faster learning and development, because the operating rhythm instils regular opportunities to debrief and adapt PDCA Learning Loops;

3. More value from coaching, because the coaches can call "plays" and discuss mindset issues, not just teach technique.

The following activities apply the principles and practices in the nets, and then in your weekly planning, to build the habit of fast adaptive learning. For more detailed examples of PDCA as a different operating rhythm for practice and matches, visit www.mindfulcricket.com and join the Mindful Cricket Community so we can share better ways to prepare for the real challenges we face in the middle.

ACTIVITY: Transform Personal Net Practice (PDCA).

This activity will help you to get familiar with PDCA thinking by using it to get the most from a net session.

. . . .

Instructions:
Choose a net session and use that to begin applying PDCA.
   Think of it in three segments batting, bowling and fielding.
   In each segment you will use the PDCA to practise mindfully.

STEP 1: Plan
Prior to the session write down two specific skills to work on during each segment. For example, in fielding it might be quick pick-up throw and taking high running catches.

STEP 2: Do
Divide up your batting, bowling and fielding time so you focus on one skill at a time.

STEP 3: Check

Pause once during each segment and at the end of each segment reflect on three questions: *What has worked? What have you learned?* and *What needs further improvement?*

If possible, get feedback from your coach or teammates.

Make a habit of taking a Centring Breath before checking in, so you keep refining your breathing as a trigger for composure and focus.

STEP 4: Adapt

Apply what you learned to improve in the next practice session or match, and then repeat the same process for each practice segment. At the end of practice, review what worked, where improvement is needed, and the next steps.

MINDFUL PRACTICE 2:
Make Adaptive Thinking a Team Habit.

Traditional cricket practice lacks the player ownership and fast feedback which is needed to build the Adapt Fast skills and mindset.

ACTIVITY: Transform Team Net Practice (PDCA).

This activity will develop your ability to learn and adapt quickly, by applying the PDCA process with a small team in a practice session.

Instructions:

Allocate approximately 120 minutes to the net session.

Form a "net team" of 6-8 players, and ensure each player has a practice journal and pen.

If you have access to a whiteboard, that will add further to the session because the transparency of seeing each other's written goals is powerful, although it's not essential.

Divide the session into segments ("sprints") during which players will Plan-Do-Check-Adapt before going again. For a group of six players across 120 minutes, the cadence is 15 minutes for planning and set up, then 20 minutes per sprint, with a 5-minute check and adapt, and a 15-minute whole of session debrief at the end.

STEP 1: Plan

Use the first 10-15 minutes for each player to choose and write down skills and practices they specifically want to work on in the session. If there is a whiteboard, post the plans on the board.

Here is a basic example:

> *Bowling:* 1 - Rhythm through the crease. 2 - Closing out an innings. 3 - Leg Cutter.
>
> *Batting:* 1 - Starting the innings. 2 - Holding shape while attacking. 3 - Defensive technique.

STEP 2: Do

Progress with the first sprint, with players working on one nominated skill at a time while coaches or the non-bowlers play the role of checking-in on what's happening and ensuring everyone is getting immediate feedback on what they're doing.

STEP 3: Check

Pause at the end of each sprint to do a fast check-in/debrief for 5 minutes, focused on three questions for each player:

What did you achieve and learn?

What's still blocking you that needs attention?

What's your next goal?

STEP 4: Adapt

Players jot any insights into journals and then get on with the next sprint.

STEP 5: Session Debrief

At the end of all the sprints, allocate 15 minutes to an overall session debrief. Have each player review their progress, seek any extra feedback, and then record what they achieved and how they will adapt in the future.

. . . .

MINDFUL PRACTICE 3:
Make Learning Loops A Life Habit.

Planning in a changeable environment means constant learning and adapting by testing what's working and what's not, and then adjusting the plan. It's much more dynamic than traditional planning.

That doesn't mean you don't need long-term goals or plans, but it's like the difference between a train and a yacht. Both have a destination, but the train has a predictable pathway, so it's easy to plan the steps. A yacht on water is affected by weather and currents, so the crew uses adaptive thinking (PDCA) to navigate to the destination.

Cricket certainly isn't as predictable as the train, so adaptive thinking using PDCA learning loops offers real possibilities to boost the way you practise and play.

ACTIVITY: Make Adaptive Thinking a Weekly Habit.

The aim of this activity is to get you into the habit of applying PDCA thinking so it becomes a natural strength in the moment-by-moment challenges of practice and matches. Accordingly, you will be setting up learning loops for your cricket based on 4 x 1-week segments (sprints) and the habit (ritual) of doing something every day to Plan, Do, Check and Adapt. Ready to give it a go?

Instructions:

To get set up, you will need the following resources to create a Performance Planning Space:

- pad of sticky post-it notes (or tear up sheets of paper into post-it sizes and get some sticky tape or Blu Tack)
- dark coloured pen
- clear space on a wall, whiteboard, piece of board or window (approximately 1.5 metres square).

When you have the resources, write "My Projects" on a post-it and place it near the top left-hand corner of your Performance Space. Next write "To Do", "In Progress" and "Done" on three other post-its and place them equal distances apart across the top of your Space, to the right of your "My Projects" post-it. You are ready to start!

Note: There is a free video at www.mindfulcricket.com which walks through this process, which is commonly called "Agile Project Management" in business.

STEP 1: Plan

Choose no more than three specific performance areas related to cricket that you'd like to improve in the next four weeks (you can add more topics and bigger detail later but let's keep it simple to begin). For example, those three might be Batting Concentration, Flexibility and Slips Catching. We will call these *Projects*.

1. **Name the Projects:** Write the names of each of the three project areas in capital letters on separate post-its and place them equally spaced down the far left-hand side of your performance space under the *My Projects* heading. Draw a line around the edge of each post-it so they will be distinguished as the project cards.

2. **Define Success:** Take each project one at a time and decide what success means for you in the next four weeks. For example, in Batting Concentration, you might decide on two success goals/measures, such as averaging above 40 over the

month, and no loss of wicket due to lapses in concentration. For Slips Catching, it could be to make ten successful catches in a row at training and catch 80% of chances. Write those goals on post-its. Add the word *Goal* at the top of each post-it and place them all next to the relevant Project card.

3. **Design your Week #1 Sprint Plan:** Ask yourself the question: *What are the most impactful tasks I can do for each project in this next week?* For example, for Batting Concentration you might decide to (a) refine your pre-game routine, (b) use Go-To-Plans for each innings, (c) practise 1-2-3 Reset at practice. Write these tasks on separate post-its and put them under the *To Do* header alongside the relevant Project. If in doubt, always go for smaller tasks and create more post-its, because a key to adaptive thinking is to take things in small bite-sized pieces.

STEP 2: Do

Choose ten minutes each day to allocate to what is called a "stand-up", where you stand in front of your Performance Space and consider what you are going to do today on your most impactful tasks. Most people do it at the start of the day, so let's assume that's your choice.

Look at each of your three Projects and decide which tasks it will be most valuable to do today. If you think some of your tasks look too big, then break them into smaller tasks and write those on other post-its. For example, if you have "Do a stretching routine" for your Flexibility project, then keep that in the *To Do* column, but on another post-it describe what exactly you'll do today (e.g. 20 minutes foam roller and core strength) and put that in the *In Progress* column.

The aim is to have only a few post-its in the *In Progress* column to describe what you'll do today. Again, if in doubt do less not more.

Now get on with it and do what you've committed to do for the day.

STEP 3: Check

Tomorrow morning, and every day in the weekly sprint, have a ten-minute stand-up meeting at the Performance Space to ask yourself four questions:

- What did I do yesterday?
- What did I learn or improve?
- What am I going to do today?
- Are there any barriers or blocks that need attention?

Move the items on the Space as they progress, which means yesterday's *In Progress* items that have been completed are moved to *Done*. Add any new *To Do* items and pull the next activities into *In Progress*.

STEP 4: Adapt

After one week, it's time to close off your first weekly sprint.

Allocate 30 minutes to review your overall progress. Look at the goals you've set for the four weeks, and consider what's been achieved and learned, and what needs to happen next.

Now repeat the PDCA loop by defining your *To Do* list for the week and continuing that rhythm.

At the end of four weeks, allocate a full hour to consider:

- Have you achieved the goals?
- What learning and development has happened over the four sprints?
- What benefits have you gained from the PDCA loops?
- What do you want to work on for the next four weeks? Many players start using their Performance Space for cricket and non-cricket planning, such as study and work.

This cycle of setting four-weekly goals, weekly sprints and daily stand-ups is proven across the world to be a fast and effective way to develop agility and adaptability for individuals and teams.

Recap of PDCA Loop.

The key to adaptive thinking is the mindset that we do better in fast-changing or uncertain environments when we navigate by learning from doing. That means thinking on your feet in shorter time frames, smaller tasks, and using the PDCA process to test and learn, just as the skipper of a yacht is continually learning and replotting their pathway.

To get the most out of the PDCA weekly sprint loops:

- Treat your challenges as projects with clearly defined outcomes (i.e. what success means)
- Use a visual display with post-its to keep it simple
- Make your rhythm or cadence for the PDCA a ritual (i.e. weekly sprints, daily stand-ups)
- Focus on completing small tasks/goals
- Learn and adapt quickly.

Here is a journal entry from a State level player who started with the PCDA process. I asked him to write out the journey he went through, and this provides a really nice example of how adaptive thinking is about learning and refining as you move forward.

PLAYER JOURNAL

When I started with PDCA, I wondered if the post-it notes and daily stand-up process was a bit over the top, and I didn't really expect a lot of value but agreed to give it a four-week test.

In the first week, if I was 100% honest, I pretty much just went through the motions. However, it was the review at the end of the first sprint that started the change.

I'd achieved very little in that first week, so I started to get a lot more specific about my daily tasks, and the momentum built from there. By week three I was putting more projects into the plan because the PDCA was just so good at getting me efficient and nimble in making improvements and getting things done.

My Performance Coach suggested we bring PDCA into the net practice, and we applied it in three ways which all had value.

First, instead of just rocking up to training and doing whatever was happening, I used my performance space to set specific practice goals and plans for batting and fielding. I never go to training now without a clear plan and I always review it as part of my daily stand-up.

Second, I tried challenging myself to think more adaptively to each bowler by creating a scenario. For example, for one of our opening bowlers my scenario might be to score quickly right from the start, while for the other it might be to get off strike. This helped with composure and keeping it simple.

My main aim is to always have a clear plan, and to use a Centring Breath before a quick check and adapt to whatever is happening.

In games, the big benefit apart from scoring more runs is that my focus is more on proactive problem solving, whereas previously I'd let things drift and see what happened. My confidence in decision making is certainly a lot better.

An unexpected sidebar is our State Coach asked me to help set up the week's training using PDCA loops, and now the whole team is applying it and doing quick reviews. The effect has been totally positive both for our cricket and as a team, because the players now take a lot more ownership of the practice and game preparation.

As you can see, this player has got a lot of personal value from PDCA loops and brought those into his team environment.

REFLECTION QUESTIONS

How can you start to bring the PDCA habit into your practice and games?

Are you ready and willing to use a Performance Planning Space?

Are there opportunities to set up new scenarios where you try plans, do quick reviews and go again?

Can you work with a partner to make this more deliberate at practice?

Key Point Summary.

- Cricket is a game of constantly thinking on your feet and adapting quickly.
- The ball, the pitch, weather, players and the game itself all bring difference. Mindful Cricket is learning and adapting so success isn't restricted to when conditions are favourable.
- The PDCA Learning Loop describes the four steps in adaptive thinking: Plan, Do, Check and Adapt.
- PDCA is a mindset and a performance rhythm. It's thinking and planning on your feet, and it's learning by doing. It is embedding action debriefing to capture the lesson learned, highlighting and celebrating success, avoiding the repeating of mistakes, and moving on from setbacks.
- Use PDCA to get more from net sessions, to be more effective in planning your week, and in building the habit of thinking on your feet.
- For a team, PDCA is a rhythm for practice to create the environment for fast learning and empowerment of players.
- At Club and Association level, PDCA is a foundation practice for leading mindfully and building a culture of self-responsibility and openness to learn.
- Play better by making PDCA a personal, team and life habit.

Pillar 2.
Play Brave

The Arena.

Have you read the speech by US President Theodore Roosevelt (1910) featuring this powerful quote?

> *The credit belongs to the man who is actually in the arena, whose face is marred by dust and sweat and blood; who strives valiantly; who errs, who comes short again and again…who at the best knows in the end the triumph of high achievement, and who at the worst, if he fails, at least fails while daring greatly.*

It is telling that Roosevelt calls out the distinction between "the man who is actually in the arena" and the spectators, or more particularly, the critics (inner and outer) who happily and safely peddle their opinions comfortable in the knowledge they are safe from failing.

Cricket isn't about the selfless bravery in the fields of war, but there's a bravery in being yourself, your best self; and in those moments when fear and uncertainty bubble to the surface, there's a choice between going into the arena to face success or failure, or holding back in the shadows. When the ball is flying around your ears, when the physical training is really tough, and when you have difficult life decisions to make, there's a place for bravery and a spirit of character which Roosevelt's words capture brilliantly.

Acts of Bravery.

Many of the greatest acts of bravery I've seen in cricket have little to do with bat and ball: Henry Olonga and Andy Flower, wearing black armbands to mourn "the death of democracy" at the hands Mugabe's Zimbabwean regime; Michael Clarke speaking for his team in the awful days following the death of Phillip Hughes; and Marcus Trescothick announcing to the world his battle over mental health. Of course, there are countless on-field examples. Do any come readily to mind for you?

Let's be clear, bravery might be easy to write about, but its main ingredients - courage and fear - are very personal and deeply woven into our psychology. If you are brave, you are feeling fear. Isn't bravery the absence of fear? No, because fear is what you feel when exposed and vulnerable and don't know what's going to happen. Bravery is facing down and going forward despite your fears, which are so often driven by the "villains" of self-doubt, fear of failure and giving up.

Mindful Cricket confronts the villains which chip away at confidence and composure, by building Play Brave practices into our Game Mindset. Let's take a moment to call out the villains and how they can needlessly hold us back in cricket and life.

VILLAIN 1: Self-Doubt.

A familiar scenario highlights how quickly self-doubt can show itself in even the best of situations:

A leg spinner with good loop and a fair amount of turn has both batsmen tied down for five overs. Midway through the sixth over, one of the batsmen unexpectedly charges down the wicket, reaches the ball on the full and slams it straight down the ground for six. Next ball, the leggie pushes it through with flatter trajectory, only to be greeted by the batsman leaning back and cracking it forward of point for another boundary. On the final ball of the over, the slightly frazzled leggie tries a wrong 'un, over pitches slightly and is lifted wide of mid-on for another six. Sixteen runs off three balls, and the leggie (and the skipper) are wondering what to do next.

As illustrated in this example, the shifting momentum of cricket means confidence is often tested, and self-doubt lurks waiting to be triggered by just this type of situation.

That means being bold and clear about who you are and what you want to achieve in cricket and beyond and refining that into a 90-day Road Map using a framework which brings together four elements of sustainable high performance.

Mindful Cricket is facing down the villain of self-doubt by Creating Your Bold Vision.

That framework is one I've used successfully with high performance across the world; and it can be a game changer, as you'll see in the next Chapter.

VILLAIN 2: Fear of Failure.

Cricket is a game of intense and continual failure. On the majority of deliveries, bowlers fail to take a wicket, batsmen fail to score a run or at least fail to hit a boundary, and fielders fail to take a catch or create a run out.

I can hear your mind whirring! Failure is a natural and essential part of the game. Batsmen inevitably fail to score, bowlers lose their line and length, and fielders misfield or drop catches. And yet we fear failure.

Why? The best place to look for answers is to ask yourself: "What do I fear losing?" The game? Maybe, but most likely your fear isn't really about losing the game, getting out, bowling poorly, or dropping a catch. It's about the consequences, particularly the fear of being seen by others to fail, or the fear of letting important people down. These fears cause many players to be tentative and focused on avoiding mistakes rather than aggressively going for it.

Mindful Cricket is letting go of the fear of losing and to instead Put It on the Line.

VILLAIN 3: Giving Up.

In my early work with aspiring Olympic athletes, a colleague gave me a list of three behaviours which they said would predict who would make it. Such an athlete would have:

- Greater commitment and effort than their peers
- Consistent work ethic and standards
- No need for approval or rewards.

There are always exceptions, but I've found this checklist very accurate. I think the reason for the accuracy is that the items predict who will put in the sustained effort, versus who will succumb to the villain of giving up.

Mindful Cricket is Holding the Tension and continuing when others are giving up.

SCENARIO: Ready for the Arena?

*The captain coach of a local club emailed me recently to share how he used the Roosevelt quote and the Play Brave mindset with his A and B grade players. He'd given everyone a copy of the speech and a **Play Brave Toolsheet** and asked them to meet after practice to discuss what it meant for them as players and as a club. Here's a section of his email I found inspiring:*

I was disappointed initially that the older players didn't take the topic seriously. However, one of our youngest players stood up in the middle of the sarcasm and said, "I don't think we play brave. We talk a big game, but we don't put it on the line, and we don't hold the tension. We just slog and cave in."

He sat down to silence, followed by some muttering from a senior player.

I decided to try a "fist of five" exercise, which meant everyone held one fist out in front of them, and then on the call of "Now" showed fingers to rate how much they agreed with the younger player's statement (1= not at all, up to 5 = totally agree). The muttering senior player, who had been disruptive for a long time, showed one finger in a gesture, while the rest of the team were all showing four or five.

We had a great conversation which led to a commitment from the players to create a Club Creed based on the Play Brave mindset. Over the past four weeks we've devoted an hour each week to setting goals, and to sharing ideas and experiences of how to get better at Putting It On The Line and Holding the Tension.

The difference has been amazing. We've had the best month in five years as a club. Our younger players are taking more leadership and you can see we've now got that courage to lose that you've written about in the book.

Thanks. It's a long journey but I can see how we've got some mindful cricketers in the making!

Let's get practical with some practices, activities and tools you can use to create your own story about Playing Brave.

CHAPTER 10

Create Your Bold Vision.

Players who play to win, do better than those who play to avoid losing. And those who proactively take on the game and their opponents, do better than those who play to avoid mistakes.

Sport psychologists know this from their basic training, and every supporter of a football team, whatever the code, knows it too! The case for "daring greatly" is compelling, but what can we do to find the inner reserve of strength to help us win the tug of war between our fears and our courage? As always, the first step is awareness.

Mindful Cricket is using awareness to approach your vision and goals with a bold mindset.

MINDFUL PRACTICE 1: True North.

Everyone knows goals are important, but few things lift and sustain performance more than the combination of bold vision and clear goals. The reason for this is all about thinking.

"True North" is a way of thinking proven to be associated with personal effectiveness and greater achievement. It brings together the inspiration of setting a bold vision (True North) for what you want to achieve, and then follow up with the clarity and step-by-step goals of the 90-Day Road Map using an ADEP framework. ADEP is an acronym which defines the four elements of high performance – Achievement, Development, Enjoyment and Partnering. This Road Map is the second Mindful Practice in this chapter.

The four Reflection Questions below are intentionally framed to highlight two different approaches to vision and goals. They focus on cricket, but you might also want to apply them to study, career or other important aspects of your life.

REFLECTION QUESTIONS

- Bold Vision: *Do you have a vision or dream of the future that really motivates you to put in time and effort to improve your game, or do you tend to take it as it comes?*
- Stretch: *Is your vision bold and beyond what is currently possible, or is it more "low bar" with few risks or stretch?*
- Clarity: *Do you regularly set and write down clear, challenging but attainable short-term to medium-term goals for your cricket, or are they vague and unrealistic?*
- Consistency: *Do you consistently use your goals to help navigate through setbacks and challenges, or do you tend to get caught up in micro-details, like obstacles and low-quality practice?*

Mindful Cricket is having a bold vision and clear goals and using your vision and goals to navigate around the inevitable blocks and barriers, just as a yachtsman uses True North to navigate their way forward.

ACTIVITY: Create Your True North.

The purpose of this activity is to identify the True North vision for your cricket and wider life. True North is your Bold Vision and gives you the clarity of direction to make plans and decisions. I recommend you do the activity for all areas of your life (e.g. study, career etc), and the instructions are based on that approach. If you'd prefer to just focus on cricket, then do so.

Instructions:

You will need a pen and a pack of post-it notes (or sheets of paper cut into approximately 30-40 post-it note sized pieces). Putting your thinking onto these small pieces will help you to be more flexible in developing and sorting ideas and priorities.

STEP 1: Identify the Most Important Areas of Your Life

Start by writing down the most important areas of your life. Write one per note and draw a border around each note so you can see these are different from the notes you will be creating in the next steps. For example, a Cricket Academy Player doing this had five areas: *Cricket, Fitness, Study, Social* and *Family*.

STEP 2: Prioritise the Areas

Sort the Important Areas notes into priority order to truly reflect what is most important to you. Be sure to choose the order which reflects your real priorities, and not what others want you to do. This is essential because you will inevitably be making trade-offs to give time and attention to one area over the other. I remember giving my final year university studies priority over cricket because, while my goal was to play First Class Cricket, my life vision for my career was to be a psychologist and that needed extra time to get through to being registered.

Prioritisation means letting go of some things in order to focus on others. This practice of letting go is a principle of mindfulness, and there are real benefits in building the habit of letting go of things that aren't so important.

STEP 3: Think Bold - Define What You Want to Achieve

On the remaining post-it notes, jot down all the things you want to achieve in each of the Important Areas.

What time horizon would you like to use for this activity? As a guide, many people and teams use two Horizons: H#1 is short-term (12 months) and H#2 is mid- to longer-term (1-3 years).

Be bold and creative. Jot one item per note to generate a spread of post-it notes with anything that comes to mind. If you struggle to think of ideas, just ask yourself the question: What will success look like?

When you've created what feels like a full list, sort them into horizons and place them together under the Important Areas notes (those you put borders around).

Can you see one or two Horizon #2 ambitions that are the most compelling "big picture" items for you? These are likely to be your True North.

Here is an example of a Development Squad Player's Journal report on this activity:

· ·

PLAYER'S JOURNAL

My True North exercise was a bit of mess to start with, but the post-it notes really helped to get my thinking clear. It took me about a month to really land the two True North items, but since then it's been amazing in getting me organised.

The first True North is to get into university and graduate with a Commerce Degree, which sets me up to work in sport as a business. That's more than three years away, but it's definitely a bold vision. The second True North is to get a contract in one of the 20/20 leagues. Writing down that vision has been really valuable in getting me focused.

I'm now using the 90-Day Road Map to map out the pathway, and I'm pretty confident both of these can happen if I put in the work and keep my mindset clear and brave.

· ·

Take a few minutes to summarise the key items in your True North, so you can align your longer-term vision and 12-month goals. The next activity is to bring those into a 90-day Road Map.

MINDFUL PRACTICE 2:
Create Your 90-Day Performance Road Map.

Some time ago I was curious to understand why some people in sport are able to sustain their energy and results over long periods of time, while others do well for a short while and then crash and burn.

I discovered four things that almost always seemed to be in place amongst people who sustained high performance. They achieved meaningful outcomes, they were developing and growing, enjoying their sport, and their relationships with key people such as coaches and teammates were positive. Those who struggled fell short in one of these areas. For example, they weren't enjoying the sport, or they weren't getting enough sense of success and achievement.

This insight led to an incredibly valuable tool to which my team gave the unglamorous title **ADEP**.

The acronym **ADEP** stands for Achievement–Development–Enjoyment–Partnering. By using these as a framework for performance planning and review, we have the most important ingredients for sustainable high performance. Let's apply it to bring your True North plan down from the sky and onto the ground.

ACTIVITY 1: Creating Your 90-Day
Performance Road Map (ADEP).

This activity guides you to create a balanced and sustainable Road Map, which takes items from your True North and brings them into short-term goals and actions which will increase the chances of success.

. . . .

Instruction:
Review the major items in your True North and use a sheet of paper or the basic *ADEP Toolsheet* from www.mindfulcricket.com to record your thoughts.

STEP 1: Achievement

Review your longer-term vision and goals, and ask yourself the basic question: What are the most important goals to achieve in the next 90 days?

For example, if your 12-month goal is to be selected for the A-grade team, then your goals in the next 90 days might be about runs or wickets to move you in that direction. To guide you in the goal-setting process, refer to the *Seven-Point Goal Setting Tool* which follows this activity.

STEP 2: Development

Now think about the new or improved skills, fitness and mental capabilities that you'll need to develop to achieve your goals. For example, doing mindfulness training might be an important development priority along with lifting your flexibility.

STEP 3: Enjoyment

Reflect on what you need to do to make the next 90 days as enjoyable and energy-giving as possible. That might mean building in recovery times or giving yourself rewards for being disciplined.

STEP 4: Partnering

Finally, think about the people who are important in helping and supporting you to achieve your goals. What will be important to do with them in the next 90 days? For example, how can you best work with your coach? What about your contribution to the team?

The ADEP Road Map is a simple and powerful way to align your True North with short-term priorities. To create clarity of direction and priorities, refine it into a one-page plan and connect it to the PDCA weekly sprints.

MINDFUL CRICKET TOOL:
Seven Point Goal Setting Tool.

The *Seven-Point Goal Setting Tool* provides a step-by-step guide to creating specific and effective goals.

Instructions:

The seven steps are outlined below, together with a simple example for each. The *Template* can be downloaded from www.mindfulcricket.com. When using this tool, make it a ritual to pause for a few moments to breathe and bring your focus calmly into the moment. It's good practice!

STEP 1: Write Down the Goal

EXAMPLE: Average at least three wickets per game.

STEP 2: Give It A Time Frame

EXAMPLE: The whole season.

STEP 3: Confirm Why It Is Important

EXAMPLE: For the team, we need this from both opening bowlers. For me, I need this level of performance and consistency to get selected in the State Team.

STEP 4: Identify Potential Blocks

EXAMPLE: Flat pitches; loss of form.

STEP 5: Current Position In Relation to Goal

EXAMPLE: Last season average was 2.5 wickets per game with inconsistency through the middle of the season.

STEP 6: Construct A Plan With Key Activities

EXAMPLE: Fitness - Achieve 10% improvement in aerobic and flexibility. Technique - Boost accuracy across spells and develop variations for flatter wickets. Mindset - Improve my rating in the four Game Mindset areas by 20%.

STEP 7: Identify Key Resources to Achieve Goal

EXAMPLE: Work with coaches and trainers on the fitness, technique and mindset. Use Mindful Cricket Journal to track progress. Use weekly sprint goals and then debrief with coaches.

Key Point Summary.

- Players who play to win, do better than those who play to avoid losing. And those who proactively take on the game and their opponents, do better than those who play to avoid mistakes.
- The case for daring is strong. However, that means letting go of the self-doubt that causes us to play small and expect the worst.
- Bold Vision is a way of thinking that is proven to lead to greater success.
- Creating a True North provides a strong sense of direction and helps with defining shorter goals and priorities.
- Sustained performance comes from achieving, developing, enjoying and partnering (ADEP).

- The ADEP 90-Day Road Map is a performance framework which helps to make the True North a reality by creating a clear plan which shows priorities and actions.
- Seven-Point Goal Setting creates specific, measurable, achievable, relevant and agreed goals (SMARTA) and is a handy reference when creating the 90-Day Road Map.

CHAPTER 11

Put It On The Line.

Some cricketers play to win the game, others play to avoid losing. Some take on the game, others play to avoid mistakes. It's all a question of whether you put it on the line or play tentatively.

Why are we tentative when we'd rather be bold? A primary reason is fear of failure, and particularly fear of being seen to fail or let others down.

Tell-tale signs of fear of failure include being overly anxious, too cautious, doing better in practice than in games, or even taking reckless risks when pressure builds.

A Clear Mind and Bold Vision will help build your skills and confidence to put it on the line in the moments that matter, and in this Chapter I want to introduce three other practices which have helped many players to take on their fear of failure:

- **Seek success over avoiding failure** to embrace the "squirm" that comes with the possibility of failing;
- **Do the brilliant basics** to build confidence and composure for the moments that matter; and
- **Defeat perfectionism and comparison** to get rid of unhelpful thoughts and motivations.

MINDFUL PRACTICE 1:
Seek Success Over Avoiding Failure.

One thing I notice about cricketers who do well in moments that matter, is how they welcome the battle and don't mind a few physical or mental bruises. Rather than being intimidated, they enjoy the challenge, and one reason for this is a mindset that isn't fixated on winning or losing, but rather on using the challenge to test themselves.

A player might say: *I want to win, and I'm prepared to risk failing.* But Mindful Cricket takes it one step further to say: *I know I'm going to fail. It's inevitable but it doesn't worry me. I'm in here to see how far I can push it and how good I can be.*

That's vulnerability, which Brene Brown (2015) defines, in her best-selling book *Rising Strong*, as follows:

> *Vulnerability is not winning or losing. It's having the courage to show up when you can't control the outcome.*

Mindful Cricket is accepting you are vulnerable in competition. You're exposed. Not only can you fail, you will fail. It will sting at times, but that's part of the game, and you're strong enough to dust yourself off and get back up again.

How do we make this vulnerability, which many see as a weakness, into a foundation for success? There are many ways to move forward, and the foundation Mindful Practices of composure and focus are key. Next is awareness of when you put it on the line and go towards success or failure, and when you are more cautious and avoid failing.

One practice I see used by players to shift their mindset in the "Put It On The Line" direction is to play with intent. They consciously set their mind towards what they want rather than what they don't want and make a point of showing it in body language and in defensive and attacking strokes. For example, good opening batsmen can leave the ball with intent just the same as they can play attacking strokes with intent.

What does "Play With Intent" mean for you when batting, bowling, fielding and keeping?

ACTIVITY: Play With Intent.

This brief mindfulness activity asks you to be aware of when you bring either a "Seek Success" or "Avoid Failure" mindset to any practice or game situation.

. . . .

Instructions:

During practice and in matches:

1. Notice when you are becoming more tentative, e.g. holding back from playing shots.
2. Observe the feeling or emotion associated with this.
3. Consider: What is your intention? e.g. putting it on the line or holding back.
4. Choose to play with intent by acting positively in ways that go towards success or failure, rather than just away from failure.

Try Fear Setting.

We know that goal setting is a key to creating an achiever mindset, but what if we applied a similar process to our fears? What if, instead of writing out what we want to happen, we do the complete opposite and describe what we don't want?

It sounds slightly crazy, and inevitably causes a few old-style cricketers to complain about being negative and overthinking, but a practice called Fear Setting is used extensively by high performers, from athletes to Wall Street traders and fighter pilots, after it was popularised by Tim Ferriss (2007), author of the *Four Hour Work Week*.

Ferriss is an avid student of high-performance practices and I highly recommend his podcast, which is one of the highest rating in the world.

Fear Setting is about facing your fears by specifically listing what you fear and what might happen as a consequence. For example, if you fear being hit all over the field in the final over of a game, then you would list the actual situation (final over, team on verge of win, you get hit for sixes or at least boundaries off every ball) and the consequences (crowd cheering, captain gets flustered, team loses, you feel like you lost the game).

This sounds ridiculous, but it works for three reasons. First, we tend to underrate ourselves and overrate opponents; second, we overrate the likelihood of a disaster occurring; and finally, by describing the consequences we often find they are bearable or not as bad as we first thought.

If you run a business, you'll just call this "risk management" and wonder why anyone wouldn't think through risks and consequences. However, in sport it's more personal when we confront our own fears.

ACTIVITY: Face Your Fears: The Fear Setting Template.

Fear Setting is about facing your fears by specifically listing what you fear and what might happen as a consequence of those fears. Tim Ferriss recommends doing this via a three-page *Template* which guides the user through four steps. You can download an adapted version from www.mindfulcricket.com

. . . .

Instructions:

Select a fear you would like to address in cricket or in wider life and try out the four steps.

STEP 1: List the Situation

On the first page, create three lists using the titles below, and put 10–20 entries each.

- Define—What are the worst things that could happen?
- Prevent—How do you prevent each from happening?
- Repair—If the worst happens, how can you fix it?

STEP 2: Identify Benefits

On the second page, make a list of the possible benefits if you are successful or partially successful.

STEP 3: Cost of Avoidance

On the third page, make a list of the costs of your inaction. In other words, if you avoid doing this thing, what might you miss out on?

STEP 4: Reflect and Decide

Take time to read and reflect on what you've written. If helpful, discuss it with a colleague or coach, and then it's up to you to make the decision whether you want to put it on the line.

. . . .

MINDFUL PRACTICE 2: Brilliant Basics.

Have you ever been to the emergency department of a large hospital? If so, you'll know it can be as busy as a train station at peak hour. Ambulances stream in, and their patients are quickly assessed by teams of nurses and doctors before orderlies shuffle them to booths, wards and operating rooms, while injections are administered, stitches and dressings applied, and lives are saved.

Dr Atul Gawande (2010) wrote the *Checklist Manifesto*, a brilliant book which carries a scary message about emergency departments. Gawande explains that doctors and nurses know what to do to save the lives of patients with life threatening conditions like heart attacks and strokes; however, they don't do it consistently and correctly. He painted the picture of a major teaching hospital where a coronary patient has less than a 50% chance of the emergency team administering the right treatment within the critical first 90 minutes - less for asthma and stroke patients.

What he described was what cricket coaches know: **even the best performers forget the basic fundamentals when there's lots happening.**

The word "basic" is key. Gawande understood that the professionals knew what to - it was just that they didn't do that reliably under pressure.

Gawande's solution was not just breathtakingly simple, but also so effective that it substantially reduced the treatment failures. And in doing so it lifted the performance and safety of emergency and operating rooms around the world. What was the solution? *Checklists* and *Team Check-ins*.

Simple checklists made all the difference to performance. Like the Vital Signs Checklist used by nurses all over the world every six hours, pulse, blood pressure, temperature, respiration and pain. These checklists described the minimum basic steps, such as hand washing before surgery. When combined with brief regular Team Check-Ins, they gave health care professionals and teams a discipline that held up under pressure.

My research into this made me wonder: what if we applied the same approach to cricket? Instead of just assuming players would do the right thing under pressure (because they know what to do), what if we used simple checklists and check-ins - applying PDCA - to help them own their space?

I called these Brilliant Basics, and the name stuck quickly.

ACTIVITY: Brilliant Basics Checklist.

Brilliant Basics are checklists describing the fundamentals for important activities, such as game preparation, starting an innings and setting up a practice session. They can be used to prepare, as a guide during activities, and to debrief performance.

· ·

Instructions:

Get familiar with the concept and use of Brilliant Basics Checklists by creating one for your own batting or bowling preparation.

Below is an example for a bowler which shows just the minimal basics.

Example of a Bowling Checklist:
1. Loosen up
2. Mark and check run-up
3. Clear Mind - breathe
4. Right line and length for batters and conditions
5. Rhythm above all else
6. Apply pressure.

Many players, coaches and teams find Brilliant Basics Checklists very helpful in calling out the fundamentals in many different situations. For example, some use them for their preparation for games, others as a quick check-in when the game gets tight. The latter makes sense because it's rarely an exceptional delivery or shot that wins the day, and more often the player who holds their nerve and does the basics really well.

Seeking Success over Avoiding Failure and Brilliant Basics are both excellent practices for leaning into challenging situations. However, sometimes the challenge isn't just about owning our space and leaning into the challenge. Instead it can start with expectations in our minds. That's why I've included the next practice on defeating perfectionism and comparison.

· ·

MINDFUL PRACTICE 3:
Defeat Perfectionism and Comparison.

The third Mindful Practice asks you to think about the expectations you set for your game. Which means reflecting on how you judge success.

A mindful approach is to be realistic, with a suitable level of stretch in your goals, and being composed and focused in the moment. The example below from an Academy Team shows how easily we can self-sabotage by having unrealistic expectations.

SCENARIO: Cricket Academy.

When Joffra was chosen in the Academy Team, it was the breakthrough he and his family had been hoping for. No one from his school had ever made it to professional level in cricket, so there were high hopes he could be the first. He resolved to do everything possible to live up to the expectations of his family, friends and community.

From the first training session his talent and work ethic were obvious to his coaches and teammates. His timing and exquisite placement made up for his small stature, and he was always first to practice and last to leave.

Joffra tried hard to do the right things, but his coaches were concerned that he was putting too much pressure on himself and, in doing so, slowing down his learning and development. It came to a head one morning, in a situation described by a batting coach:

We did a range hitting session, which basically meant hitting balls from the centre of the oval over the infield to the boundary or beyond. It was important practice for an upcoming 20/20, where we wanted to be clear in our minds and plans about where and how to hit the ball in the air.

The top six batters took their turns, with Joffra the last to go. The five batters before him had all cleared the fence more than once, and while that's not essential, I could see Joffra was determined to do the same.

He swung so hard at the first ball that he almost fell over, but the ball barely went off the wicket square. Everyone except Joffra laughed. On the next two balls he swung hard again but was gripping the bat so hard, and losing his shape, so there was no power at all.

I walked over and asked him a few questions about his intent for the drill and his shape. His teammates were a bit loud in their banter and you could see he was embarrassed and humiliated and wasn't really listening to me.

I suggested he chip or place the final three balls into the outfield gaps, but he hit the fourth ball head high to mid-wicket and just swung wildly again at the final two.

It was a tough session for Joffra, but it opened up the conversation we needed to have with him about perfectionism and comparison. I'm sure in the future we will all look back and see that lesson was far more useful to him than trying to find a way to monster the ball out of the park.

GRANDSTAND VIEW

· What do you think the coach meant by "perfectionism and comparison", and why the lesson would be so useful for Joffra?

· How would you approach the coaching of a player like Joffra?

· What would you do about the players mocking him? Is this just part of being in a team environment, or is it unacceptable in a modern team?

Understanding Perfectionism.

There are many types of perfectionism, but at the core is the need to be seen by others as perfect or flawless. That need creates a lot of motivation, so it has value; but it also has a cost, which is often felt in unhelpful stress and anxiety.

A perfectionist might say they want to perfect something or achieve excellence; however, the underlying driver is usually not about the task itself, but more about a harsh inner critic and meeting the approval (or avoiding the disapproval) of other people.

Joffra's behaviour highlights three core characteristics of perfectionism:

1. Setting impossibly high standards
2. Getting overly upset when making a mistake
3. Distorted view of priorities.

These three elements cause lots of stress and involve hard work. Yet for the perfectionist nothing is ever good enough, which means their enjoyment is fleeting at best.

REFLECTION QUESTIONS

Do you recognise any perfectionism in your mindset?

Do mistakes make you angry or frustrated?

Do you tend to put more weight on other people's opinions than your own?

Do you often make comparisons with others?

Do you feel driven to prove yourself?

Is there an opportunity to chat with a coach or adviser who could help take off some of that pressure?

The Costs.

Perfectionists tend to avoid doing things they don't do well, which means they build on their strengths but don't properly address weaknesses unless they can do it in private. Have you seen batsmen do this by refusing to address their difficulties with the short ball and endlessly pounding drives into the net?

Perfectionists get upset more easily when decisions go against them. They can let a poor umpiring decision or a dropped catch affect their enjoyment and performance for the rest of the game, whereas a mindful approach is to let it go.

Understanding Comparison.

Accompanying perfectionism is the tendency of players to compare themselves with others and to over-emphasise gaps and weaknesses. This can be a vicious circle because the feeling of inferiority drives the player to further hide their weaknesses and vulnerabilities, when that's exactly what's needed to open up and improve.

If this topic resonates for you, you are in very good company. A significant percentage of top performers have a tendency towards perfectionism and/or comparison, and some will argue it's an important contributor to their success. They are right to a point, because a moderate level of perfectionism or comparison does help to set high standards and put in the work. However, when good enough is never good enough, it can be self-defeating.

The player with a strong motivation to gain approval by showing they are better than others, is on an impossible journey, whereas one who looks to compare in order to learn is far more realistic.

If you do find this topic applies to you, then have a conversation with your coach or team psychologist about the difference between being motivated to achieve realistic and stretch goals, and being driven to prove yourself to others. The latter means the value you put on yourself is always conditional on how you are performing and on how you compare with others, while the former is under your control.

Mindful Cricket is about learning to accept your unique self for who you are and what you are today - not in comparison with others.

ACTIVITY: Mindful Practices and Tools for Perfectionism.

The whole Game Mindset framework has the potential to reduce the damaging effects of perfectionism by building your emotional balance and sense of self. Accordingly, here is a brief reminder of some of those practices.

Instructions:

Take a moment to reflect on how the Game Mindset practices can help to reduce the damaging effects of perfectionism and comparison:

- The **Clear Mind** concepts of Composure, Focus in the Moment and Keep it Simple each play a role in reducing the pressure that comes from perfectionism. Practices such as centring, quietening the inner critic and simple plans foster a different energy and attention so you can play mindfully, instead of feeling driven to standards that are unrealistic and damaging.
- **Adapt Fast** helps by setting smaller more realistic goals and using the PDCA Learning Loop to achieve outcomes and make learning and improving a habit.
- The **Play Brave** practice of the 90-Day Road Map (ADEP) is a great foundation, because thinking about what "enjoy" means

to you and choosing your "develop" priorities will help to bring more fun and more growth, rather than what we saw with Joffra. He certainly wasn't having fun, and that's one clear sign of a perfectionist.

- The **Play Clever** and **Play Better** sections of the book offer a range of practices to bring you back to the Brilliant Basics and to be realistic in setting goals and debriefing and evaluating your performances.

To close off this detailed but important topic, here's the Brilliant Basics Checklist, which summarises the approach the coach co-created with Joffra.

Brilliant Basics Checklist – Joffra.

1. Be clear about goals, e.g. develop shot making to keep the score moving in the 20/20 middle overs
2. Reduce unrealistic standards, e.g. play to strengths and expect to learn from things that don't work
3. Call out what you do well, e.g. placement, fast running, turning over the strike.

SCENARIO: A Final Word from the Academy Coach.

I'm delighted to say that Joffra has really turned things around. He's stopped comparing himself to the big hitters and has realised his value to the team is as the "rock" around which other players build the innings. He's watched how Joe Root and Steve Smith play these roles in their 50 over teams, and he's becoming much more open about putting himself in positions to learn, when he would have just got upset previously.

Key Point Summary.

- Mindful Cricket is bringing a mindset of enjoying the challenges and a desire to test yourself, rather than being fixated on winning and losing.
- Vulnerability is fundamental to putting it on the line. It's having the courage to turn up.
- Even the best performers forget the basics when under pressure. That's where Brilliant Basics are simply brilliant.
- Instead of worrying about fears, try a Fear Setting exercise to really draw out what you are fearing, and see if it is as bad as you imagined.
- Perfectionism takes the fun out of the game and creates tension and anxiety that is counterproductive.
- Put value on yourself for who you are, not how many runs or wickets you are taking.
- Game Mindset provides a host of practices to help reduce the costs of perfectionism and comparison.

CHAPTER 12

Hold The Tension.

Batsmen fight their way through tough patches, bowlers work to a plan which is overs in the making, and fielders sustain the pressure throughout a long partnership. Cricket rewards those who persevere.

In a meeting with the Australian Test Squad prior to an overseas tour, we reviewed a string of recent Tests where strong batting and bowling positions were lost in just a few overs by the fall of quick wickets or leaking runs.

In consecutive Tests when the team was batting they were in the vicinity of 160 for 2 in the middle session, with an aim of around 320 by stumps. The plan was to have established batsmen still in so they could bat well into the second day and then build scoreboard pressure on the opposition with attacking fields. Good strategy. However, on both occasions they lost three wickets around the tea break, and struggled to stumps, barely reaching 300 before being dismissed early the next day.

It was a similar story when they were in the field. They'd won or broken even in most sessions however, when they did lose a session, it was a big loss.

A debriefing discussion on these experiences led to a plan and agreed tag line called 'Hold the Tension', which was about understanding and shaping the momentum of the game.

MINDFUL PRACTICE 1:
Shape the Momentum.

Next time you watch a game of cricket, observe which team is applying the pressure at any given moment.

Look for signs the batsmen are stuck on strike, the run rate has slowed, or the fielding team is bringing a lot of energy to the game:

How do the batsmen handle being bogged down?

Do they work the strike by pushing quick singles, do they take calculated risks and chip over the infield, or do they go for big shots?

The fundamental issue is how they respond to the tension building in their minds and bodies. If the tension is taking over, you might see it in the batsman's body language, such as losing their physical shape as they try to overhit the ball, or perhaps a bad call for a run.

Let's assume the momentum shifts towards the batsmen. An early sign of tension in the bowlers might be inconsistency in line or length. Bowlers feeling the pressure often strive harder for a wicket, which causes actions to come unbalanced and rhythm lost. Watch them looking at the footmarks, querying the state of the ball, or just shrugging their shoulders when a slightly false shot is played to a good delivery.

Cricket is a game of momentum and can switch back and forth in less than an over. Players shape the momentum in all manner of ways. Skilful short form batsmen target the short boundary and break up the bowling plan with just a couple of well hit sixes. Opening batsmen leave anything wide or short and frustrate a fielding side who won the toss and expect wickets. And, of course, two quick wickets will change any game.

The key to shaping the momentum is to Hold the Tension so you are in a position to move when the opportunity arises.

Choose Short-Term Goals.

I once interviewed the Chief Commander of an elite Military Special Forces Group. We discussed the mindset and tools used in battle, and the Chief immediately went to what he called Short-Term Goals.

He explained how in the heat of battle, when momentum can mean life or death, soldiers must make clear, rational decisions despite the tension in their minds and bodies. He suggested the single most important mindset tool to shape momentum was setting very short-term and specific goals, such as moving successfully from one room to another in an urban conflict or shifting the sniper position to get a clearer overview in mountainous terrain. Short-Term Goals increase focus and build confidence as they are achieved.

Momentum shifts quickly in war and in cricket, which makes it important to Hold the Tension so we take the right action at the right time. For the soldier, that's the timing to move forward, and for the cricketer it's the timing of deliveries and shots (which we explore further in *Absorbing and Applying Pressure* in the next Section). Short-Term Goals are fundamental to shaping the momentum.

ACTIVITY: Short-Term Goals.

In any situation where you are feeling pressured, a well-chosen Short-Term Goal can provide the focus and confidence you need to persist towards your overall objective.

Instruction:

Start with setting goals in practice, by building them into your Go-To-Plans. For example, when bowling set yourself a target for each six deliveries, such as drawing the batsman into a mistimed stroke; or when batting you might set yourself to work two deliveries in every six into areas where you could run a single.

In game situations get into the habit of setting short-term targets, so they are natural to use when under pressure. Here are a few examples:

- Bowl a maiden
- Break up the field with quick singles
- Get through to the end of the power play
- Move the team in 10 run increments
- Create a run out chance.

Be deliberate in choosing specific Short-Term Goals to maintain your focus and to shape momentum when the tension is building.

Surrender Control.

Does that sound impossible? It certainly isn't an easy practice to grasp. Driving a car is a good example of this mindset, and of why it works well in semi-chaotic environments. As you drive through traffic there are things to control and things to let be. You can't control what other drivers do, or the layout of the road and intersections, and if you do allow your mind to be preoccupied with those things, you risk losing attention on what you can control - the direction, pace and positioning of your car. If you are constantly expecting a crash, or demanding other people drive the way you do, you'll likely increase the chances of an accident because your heightened (uncomfortable) feelings might cause you to make a bad decision.

Mindful Cricket is shaping the momentum while surrendering overall control.

In cricket there are many things which can trigger frustration or agitation. Mindful Practices like *Centred Breathing* help us to accept these as they are rather than complaining of what is happening or worrying over what might happen. I've seen many international batsmen successfully develop this mindset, and you might sense it when they say their mental approach is to clear their mind and trust their instincts.

ACTIVITY: Mental Rehearsal: Let Go - Welcome the Squirm.

This activity uses visualisation or imagery techniques to build on your mindful relaxation and meditation practices and is more advanced than most of the activities in the book. It is included to highlight the opportunity for you to make a subtle shift in your mindset about conditions or situations that bother or distract you.

. . . .

Instruction:

Think about situations which cause you to get frustrated or agitated. These might be in cricket or wider life. For example, in cricket it might be when the pitch is a bit uneven, the wind annoyingly blustery or you've just had two catches dropped in the past two overs.

Go through your usual Centred Breathing practice for a few minutes to settle the busy mind.

When ready, in your mind call up the image of one of the situations where the uncomfortable feelings have arisen. Use your imagination to see the situation and to feel the emotions as if you were in the middle of the situation right now.

While continuing with the Centred Breathing, observe the feeling, give it a label (frustration, annoyance, etc) and then imagine yourself getting right through it without responding to the feeling and instead just letting it roll over you.

Run the scene a few times and work with the mindset of just accepting things as they are. That doesn't mean ignoring them, because you don't ignore the bad drivers on the road or difficult situations in a game; however, it is your choice how you respond to your own emotions. And yes, it's not the situation you are responding to, it's your emotions, which of course are being triggered by your thinking.

. . . .

We live in a world we don't control. No doubt we can influence things, but it's incredibly stressful to try controlling everything. Letting go and surrendering a little control is a Mindful Practice which takes time to develop, but the benefits in less stress and greater composure are worth seeking.

MINDFUL PRACTICE 2: Get Above the Noise.

You've heard more than once that personal change and adaptability require three steps: awareness, then acceptance and finally action. Awareness is the gateway to the other two.

As tension builds, we risk losing awareness, because it's hard to think clearly when you're overwhelmed by feelings like anxiety, frustration or impatience. Without awareness, players grip the bat harder, make poorer and more reactive choices, and drop into the red zone.

Tension acts like noise and it's hard to get perspective. **Mindful Cricket is about being aware of signs that you are dropping into the red zone and then finding ways to get above the noise and get the perspective needed to make intelligent choices.**

ACTIVITY 1: Get in the Grandstand.

This activity is all about having the self-awareness to step back from the "noise" of competition and thinking from a different perspective.

Instruction:

When we experience setbacks and disappointments on the field of play (or life) it is easy to be caught up in feelings of self-pity, loss and helplessness. However, a mindful approach is to step back, take a breath and think from a different perspective. It's like stepping off the field and taking a few moments to view things clearly from the grandstand.

"Get in the Grandstand" means pausing for a moment, taking a breath and separating yourself from the action and noise. It's the mindful skills we've already covered to slow it down, quieten the noise and reflect: *What's happening here?* and *What's my best choice?*

Sometimes it's very hard to get a detached perspective, so having a coach or friend help you can be a useful strategy. Of course, in the middle of a game you can't ask a coach, but that's where partnerships are so important.

Probably the most effective tool that the Australian Test Team used to make Hold the Tension a winner was communication in partnerships. The batsmen committed to be direct and honest with teammates when they saw early signs of tension. They became mindful of changes in each other's rituals or signs that the batting shape was shifting. They helped their teammates get the "grandstand perspective" so they could reset and not play a false stroke.

The bowlers also worked in partnership, along with the keeper, to apply pressure through the line and length they wanted to each batsman.

Hold the Tension was just one small part of the overall jigsaw. However, the Team averaged closer to 400 across the next series, and the number of times the opposing batsmen got control of momentum reduced. They also got better at noticing when their opponents were struggling to Hold the Tension, and that created more opportunities.

GRANDSTAND VIEW

Take a few minutes now to sit in the grandstand and ask yourself these three questions:

- Where are you feeling stress or pressure in your cricket or life?
- What signs in your thinking or behaviour would be signals that you are losing focus, confidence or discipline?
- What mindful actions can you take to address this constructively?

ACTIVITY 2: Ask for Help.

Whether the tension you feel is coming from sport, study, work or life, it's valuable to have trusted friends or support to help you work through the difficult issues. Coaches, doctors, physical trainers, psychologists and mentors all play this role at times in professional teams.

Instructions:

Cricketers (and men in particular) aren't good at asking for help because many are conditioned to think any sign of vulnerability is weakness. Interestingly, there is not a shred of evidence to suggest vulnerability is a sign of character weakness, and in fact there's plenty of research to suggest exactly the opposite.

Being open to sharing your feelings, including doubts and uncertainties, is a doorway to growth and self-confidence, whereas acting out "toughness" is a defensive play which makes you weaker.

- What issues would you benefit from discussing with a trusted person?
- Who can you find to help you with perspective?

Choose an issue and give it a go. You'll likely be surprised what a stress reliever it can be.

MINDFUL PRACTICE 3:
Defeat Self-Sabotage.

In a game of persistence, where Holding the Tension is essential, the ability to stick to the fundamentals and maintain positive energy is vital. We've seen the effect of not doing the Brilliant Basics, where highly skilled people undermine their own efforts.

I've seen many players self-sabotage their own performance, in preparing to play and in matches. The causes are many and varied; as always, however, awareness is the starting point to check on things like sleep, nutrition, mindful meditation and daily rituals, which can make or break success.

ACTIVITY: Defeating Self-Sabotage.

This activity is designed to help you climb into the grandstand to identify and defeat unhelpful habits which might be holding you back and sabotaging your efforts.

. . . .

Instructions:

Follow the **four steps to avoid self-sabotage:**

1. **Identify the behaviours**
2. **Control your environment**
3. **Be accountable**
4. **Get it done.**

These four simple steps can be applied to things you do on a daily basis, or to specific situations that happen in matches. Give them some thought and if needed, chat with your coach to get their ideas and input.

STEP 1: Identify the Specific Behaviours

Are there areas in your life where you are ill-disciplined or self-sabotaging? For example, is it nutrition, showing up late, playing 'get out' shots?

Jot down your answers and see if you can spot a pattern of behaviour and/or specific areas that would benefit from attention.

STEP 2: Control Your Environment

We often inadvertently make life hard for ourselves by creating an environment which encourages self-sabotage. For example, if your aim is to stick with good nutrition, then remove the tempting snacks; or if you need more loosening and stretching, then don't arrive to training at the last minute.

Reflect on the areas in your 90-Day Road Map where you've identified priorities to develop.

As you think of each area, consider whether you are creating the ideal environment for success. For example, for Centred Breathing, do you put your smartphone on silent and choose a distraction-free time and place, or do you just take your chances?

STEP 3: Be Accountable

For goals which might be open to ill-discipline and distraction, it can be valuable to tell other people your goal. Public commitment increases the chances of success because you have more on the line.

STEP 4: Get it Done

There is a strategy in personal development called "fake it until to you make it", which essentially means do the behaviour and act it out until the habit is formed. As the Nike advertisement says, *Just do it.* Many people use old-style self-discipline to do what's needed irrespective of whether they feel like it or not.

· ·

It works for doing physical training, so are there other areas where you could simply commit to doing the behaviour and/or maintaining the standard?

Key Point Summary.

- Batsmen fight their way through tough patches, bowlers work to a plan which is overs in the making, and fielders sustain the pressure throughout a long partnership. Cricket rewards those who persevere by Holding the Tension.
- Cricket is a game of momentum and it can switch back and forth in less than an over. The key to shaping the momentum is to Hold the Tension so the game moves in the direction you want.

- Set and work towards Short-Term Goals to provide focus and build self-confidence.
- Be mindful of what you can control, and what just takes away energy and concentration, and is therefore best to let go.
- When you feel tension building, take a brief pause (breath) to dial down the "noise" and to think from a different perspective.
- Ask for help.
- Defeat self-sabotage by creating the environment around you which drives commitment and action.

The Player's Journal below is a delightful summary of the whole Play Brave section and highlights how adopting these Mindful Practices can help create a Game Mindset that is unique and effective.

· ·

PLAYER'S JOURNAL

Hi Me ☺

Hasn't Play Brave been a game changer! Remember how I was doubting myself, scared of failing and ready to give up and try another sport? Those villains described me to a tee.

Well things can and do change!

Mindful Cricket opened my eyes to two BIG learnings:

First, it's MY mindset, not the game of cricket that needed changing.

Second, there are small steps I could take to make a big difference in how I think and feel.

It seems ages ago that I started with the True North and ADEP tools. It took a couple of weeks to get really clear what's important. That was less about cricket and more about how to get priorities sorted between sport, study and work.

Putting the Performance Space on my wall was a winner. I can see my goals and I can see my progress. Wow! Progress every day on the little goals just makes things so much easier.

I'd be lying if I said I wasn't still battling with the fear of failure, but I've put together Brilliant Basics Checklists for batting, bowling and game preparation, and that's been helpful in framing things more optimistically.

Those words "Hold the Tension" have become my mantra. It's not so much having a practice as having a mindset trigger to fall back on when mind drift happens.

I actually like me a lot better now! Yep ... there is a perfectionist in there but it's not driving the vehicle like it was a few weeks ago.

There's plenty left to do but hey – I've made more runs and taken more wickets in the past six weeks than ever before. That's not what really matters though. I'm just better set up to be the ME I WANT TO BE!!!!

Pillar 3.
Play Clever

Clever or Dumb?

Cricketers waste countless opportunities because they don't think clearly and cleverly in matches. Teams throw away finals or miss opportunities because bowlers fail to adapt their length to suit the conditions, and batsmen give away their wickets on the cusp of victory.

Disappointed players wonder if they really do have talent or ability, and usually the response is more planning or go back to the nets. What if the problem wasn't about ability, but how smart or clever we are in using our abilities in dynamic, fast changing situations?

Many cricketers don't rate the skill of Playing Clever as much as they rate the skill of forward defence or taking a slips catch. Typically, they arrive at practice, grab a ball and start bowling. If they beat the bat, they feel good, and if their best deliveries get hit they start fiddling with their action and run-up. Batsmen pad up, stroll into the nets and start playing shots, often oblivious to what the outcome of the shot might have been on a cricket ground. That's not Mindful Cricket - that's mindless cricket.

Mindless Cricket.

Sadly, a significant percentage of cricket training is mindless, dumb cricket. It is physical and technical preparation but it's not training the mind to play the game of cricket. Instead it is training the mind to play the technical skills of cricket.

Disagree if you like. However, take 10 minutes to watch a bowler in a match and imagine what's happening in their mind:

Are they nervous?

Can you see them feeling out the conditions and reacting to the consequences of their bowling?

Are they getting wickets?

Who's in control... batsmen or bowlers?

What field placing is needed?

How to stop the single?

What about the dropped catch?
Wickets falling or not falling as expected?
And so on...

Mindful bowling is being clever enough to know your game, and to read the momentum and challenges of the game as it unfolds. Now watch a bowler in the nets:

What are they doing, and more particularly what are the consequences of their bowling?
How different are the conditions to the demands in a match?
Are they working on tactics or technique?
Are they simulating the rhythm of overs and changes of batsmen or just bowling to one batsman?
Are they Absorbing And Applying Pressure or going through the motions?

Cricket is played above the shoulders, and we know that because we watch mindless cricket and see it beaten time and again by cricket smarts. Clever bowling with subtle pressure and variation draws the batsman into a false stroke. Mindless batting overreaches and gets out early on a day when runs were just waiting to be had.

We can learn to play clever cricket. It's not a fixed ability. This is about thinking, and we can sure change that by being aware of our strengths, style and limitations, and by better understanding and reading the game.

Smart Cricket.

The pillars of Clear Mind and Play Brave give you every chance of playing to your potential; however, to get the full benefits of composure, clarity, adaptability and a Bold Mindset requires you to play a clever game.

To Play Clever, we deep dive into three chapters covering Bat Smart, Bowl Smart, and Keep and Field Smart, where you'll learn the value of Smart

Basics, the skills of Adaptability and Partnering, and how to Absorb and Apply Pressure.

The themes of Know Your Game and Read the Game are woven throughout:

Know Your Game *is playing to your strengths and being aware cricket is a game played inside limitations. It's not the downhill skier on the edge of disaster, but more the Formula One driver holding shape and control while avoiding the overreach.*

Read the Game *is understanding the conditions and the momentum and playing with tactics and pressure in every game situation. It's knowing what to do and when to do it.*

See the connection? If you can't read the game you can't apply your strengths and skills to maximum effect, and if you don't know your style, strengths and limitations you won't be able to execute on your clever plans and tactics.

Ready to Play Clever?

Excited? Imagine the possibilities when you have a sound foundation of daily habits and rituals built on Brilliant Basics and are ready to bring your strengths to play in the right situation at the right time in the right way.

That's a Mindful Cricketer who knows how to Play Clever.

CHAPTER 13

Bat Smart.

The foundation practices of Clear Mind and Play Brave give you every chance of playing to your potential, but the full benefits of great preparation and a Bold Mindset come by playing a clever game. Too many players never reach those heights because they don't know that feeling comfortable with your game requires knowing your game and knowing the game.

In this chapter you'll explore **four practices which hold the key to smart batting**:

1. **Smart Batting Basics** is about building trust in your basics and knowing how to bring them consistently to your game. Those basics include *starting smart, batting in different positions in the order* and *holding your shape*.

2. **Adapt to Change** is a brief overview of how to adapt to different pitch conditions, and types of bowling.

3. **Create Partnerships** discusses the importance of partnerships and how to use them to gain an edge.

4. **Absorb and Apply Pressure** begins by reflecting on situations that create pressure for you and how to bring Mindful Cricket Practices and tools into play. We then flip the picture and look at the opportunities to apply pressure when batting.

MINDFUL PRACTICE 1:
Smart Batting Basics.

A mindful batsman feels comfortable and confident playing their game in moments that matter.

What does "moments that matter" mean to you? What sort of game situations matter? I asked a 20-year-old batsman this question recently and they nominated three situations which have arisen for them in the past few games:

- starting an innings
- when momentum shifted
- final overs of a match.

In these moments that matter, it becomes even more important than ever to trust your basics, because that's what holds things together. Let's explore five that matter.

BASICS 1: Start Smart with Intent.

Arguably the most difficult aspect of batting is starting your own innings, because unlike most sports, one small error of judgement in cricket can see you quickly back in the change rooms.

Starting Smart is all about consistent trusted pre-performance rituals, so be sure to get these sorted and make them part of your Brilliant Basics.

Unless your game plan and strengths are suited to all-out attack from the outset, the smartest option is to play within your limitations early in your innings. Take time to assess the conditions and the strengths and limitations of the bowlers. This doesn't mean being passive, it means playing with intent.

Use every opportunity in practice and games to experiment with what Playing With Intent means for starting your innings. As with every aspect of the game, it's individual. For example, Glen Maxwell and Kane Williamson might both start their innings by playing with intent, but they won't be batting the same way. The similarity will be in clear intention, which for

Maxwell might mean taking on the bowler, whereas Williamson is more likely looking to work the ball into gaps and rotate strike as he fully judges pace and bounce.

Always be mindful that a smart start isn't so much about runs. It's about what suits your game and the conditions, so you are there to shape the momentum as the game unfolds.

BASICS 2: Bat Smart in Your Position.

What position in the order do you usually bat? Each position has its own special demands and tactics, which are further influenced by the state of the game. Here are a few reminders of the intent you might see in the various positions.

Opening: Smart openers expect bowlers to be fresh at the start of the innings, so they aim to stay composed and courageous in the face of intimidation from the quicks. Their intent is often to take advantage of gaps in an attacking field by looking for singles from defensive strokes, and for boundaries when the opportunity arises. They know they'll get some unplayable deliveries but there will also be opportunities in some games to build their innings long after the initial onslaught.

Number Three: The "first-drop" or number three position in First Class teams is often reserved for the best batsman in the side. The theory is that this position offers the best player some protection against the new ball, while also giving the opportunity for a lengthy stay at the crease.

Smart number threes are positive and adaptable in their intent. They'll be mentally ready to bat from the second ball of the game, knowing the role might be to consolidate the team's position and avoid an early collapse, or it could be to build on a strong start.

Middle Order: The term "middle order" refers to the batting positions from four to seven, usually occupied by batsmen or all-rounders (including the wicket-keeper). The smart middle order game is built on partnerships to capitalise on a good start, or to rebuild after the earlier batsmen have been dismissed. Two or three stroke-makers and someone who can play the "anchor role" is a common middle order structure. Adaptability is also essential, to face a relatively new ball at times, and at other times bat late in the innings when quick runs are needed.

The Lower Order: Many matches are won or lost by less than the number of runs scored by the last four batsmen, so for this reason alone Smart Batting means the lower order practise their skills, and have the intent to contribute runs, or to defend while a recognised batsman scores.

REFLECTION QUESTIONS

If you open, what's your usual intent in the first 5-10 overs?

If you bat at number three, what intent do you bring?

If you bat in the middle order, how well do you adapt to different situations?

If you bat in the lower order, what intent do you typically bring?

BASICS 3: Hold Your Batting Shape.

Athletes across a wide range of sports proactively train their minds and bodies to reliably own their space and hold their shape in the moments that matter. Here are some examples:

Snooker players *have a training drill where they lay an empty glass bottle on the table and practise stroking the cue stick through the neck of the bottle over and over without touching the bottle. It requires precision and it builds trust in the most important basic in snooker – a consistent stroke. This practice drill is about learning to trust mind and body to create the shape of the shot.*

Tennis players *want to strike the ball with the power of their whole body and to trust the shape of their shot under pressure. You'll see the top players drill their backhands and forehands as a whole-body exercise, taking care to get head position, hip and shoulder alignment and balanced footwork all coming together in a coordinated way.*

Golfers want to trust and hold their body shape under pressure, so they work on whole body shape in their swing. They know that relying on small muscles in wrists and forearms creates an unreliable swing which falters under pressure. They'll know when it works because of feel and sound.

The greatest batsman of them all, Don Bradman, practised for countless hours with a stump and golf ball. Not only that, he used a water tank to bounce the ball off. He learned how to shape his body to control a fast and erratic ball. It was an unorthodox technique, yes, but he was sixty percent better than any other player in history. He trusted and held his shape under pressure. Do you trust yours?

Recall the drills in *Focus in the Moment*. Do you remember the Touch, Feel and Rhythm drill of listening for the sound of a well-timed shot? It's a great drill because it's only going to happen consistently when you hold your shape.

Lose shape and you lose power. Watch batsmen closely to see what happens. Some fall over slightly to the offside, some reach out too far for the ball, or flick off balance at a wide ball. Another common sight is the batsman caught in "no man's land" against a spinner, neither fully forward nor fully back. They're off balance and vulnerable to a range of possible dismissals.

ACTIVITY: Hold Your Batting Shape.

This activity is a reminder of the importance of setting up your space, and then holding your shape no matter what the conditions.

Instruction:

Get with your coach and agree to work relentlessly on knowing and holding your shape in defence and in forcing shots. Make it your intent to impose your shape on the game.

- Be comfortable and settled in your stance and rituals, because that's your space.

- Build trust in your defence. Know what a straight bat feels like in your whole body and practise it like the snooker player, with some Bradman moves (or the modern-day almost equivalent, Steven Smith) thrown in to dynamically test your balance when the ball spins, swings, dips or climbs sharply.
- Build trust in your core control. Try batting with your feet together and no footwork, so you have to work at holding your middle and upper body shape. Sound ridiculous? It is if you do it too much, but it's a good exercise to force you to retain control of your basic shape when hitting balls coming at you in all sorts of different ways.

. . . .

Mindful Cricket is setting up your space (stance and rituals) and then knowing your shape, trusting your shape and knowing what to do to get your shape back when things get unbalanced and ragged.

Can you Hold Your Shape?

BASICS 4: Bat in the Moment.

Mindful batting is batting in the moment. It is watching the ball closely and playing, or leaving, according to position and trajectory. If only it were as easy as that!

There are plenty of challenges, but a mindful approach avoids many concentration errors which cost batsmen their wicket:

- Failing to notice changes in field positions
- Being distracted by the comments of players or the crowd
- Playing a lazy defensive shot
- Thinking too much instead of playing the ball on its merits
- Misreading the type of delivery.

Smart Batting has a rhythm or cadence based on using the regular breaks between deliveries to relax (breathe) and then refocus on the job at hand.

Use the 1-2-3 Reset as a ritual to minimise the mind drift which often affects batsmen once they are settled in.

BASICS 5: Run Smart.

Running between wickets gets less attention during practice than it deserves.

Smart running starts with being a good judge of a run, which enables you to both apply pressure and reduce pressure. Smart cricket is then recognising a dip in concentration or a bowler getting on top and being alert to the possibility of a quick run. It's noting the position of the fielders, whether they are right-handed or left-handed, and if they have a strong arm.

As mentioned earlier, when two batsmen are clear in their decisions and strong in communication, they can run on just about anything.

> **REFLECTION QUESTIONS**
>
> *How clear and decisive is your running between wickets?*
>
> *Do you spend time practising running between wickets?*
>
> *Are there regular drills at practice to test your judgement and communication with teammates?*
>
> *If not, why not?*

Good running breaks up the bowler's plan and the opposing captain's field placings.

SCENARIO EXAMPLE.

In a short form match the fielding captain, concerned with the run rate, precisely sets their infield on the edge of the circle to cut off boundaries. The batsmen, noting the change, steal quick singles with shots played to just a few metres away from almost every ball of the next two overs. The pressure mounts further as the bowlers get frustrated. The batsmen are winning the momentum game when the captain reacts by bringing in two fielders. The batsmen adjust again, enjoying the lower risk of chipping over the infield.

We've explored five Basics including Starting Smart, Holding Your Shape, and Smart Running. Let's take those a step further and think about how to adapt cleverly to the ever-changing conditions and the game itself.

MINDFUL PRACTICE 2: Adapt to Change.

Cricket is a sport which requires players to constantly adapt to changing conditions. That's why Adapt Fast is a foundation principle. Let's touch on a few of the basics which are vital to Batting Smart.

Adapt to Conditions.

Adapting to pitches and ground conditions is essential, yet even the best international teams perform so much better in their home conditions. New Zealand are hard to beat on their slow seaming tracks and cool conditions, India and Sri Lanka thrive on dry turning decks, and Australians and South Africans like bounce and pace on sunny dry days.

> **REFLECTION QUESTIONS**
> *Do you play most of your cricket on turf or hard wickets?*
> *And what about those backyard or courtyard games or beach cricket?*
> *What differences do you experience across these surfaces?*
> *What about weather conditions? Do you play regularly with overcast skies or is it hot, sunny and dry?*

Adapting to different conditions is as much a mindset as it is physical. Batting Smart in different conditions starts with being mindful of the conditions and what that means to get the percentages in your favour. Talk with your coach and experienced players to learn their strategies.

If the new ball is swinging, then the key is to negate the danger of late swing. Some players bat out of their crease, while others stay back and play as late as possible. Reverse swing brings slightly different risks, particularly if there is a late dip into the stumps. A smart play is to be precise in the angle of your backlift so you don't get trapped playing late and across the line. Also be clear in your intent to get outside the line with definite footwork. Similarly, with turning tracks, getting the bat out in front of the pad and quick footwork are essential to avoid losing shape and playing off balance in that halfway position.

With understanding of the Basics, the next step is to set up practice drills so you can simulate the challenges and learn how to set strategies that leverage your basics and work in your favour.

PRACTICE SCENARIO:

To prepare their team for a series of games in India, where sharp and at times unpredictable turn was expected, the coaches set up a series of drills including putting gravel on a practice pitch and throwing into the area so batsmen could practise getting their mindset and technique settled.

By experiencing the unpredictable turn (which replicated the turn from footmarks and worn patches), the batsmen learned to keep a Clear Mind, to stay composed and to work to simple plans.

Initially most reacted by just pushing harder at the ball, but soon they started using their feet, being more confident in sweeping and moving precisely back and forwards. They also learned to focus one ball at a time and to dismiss thoughts of the extreme bounce or spin. Importantly, they came to trust that if they held their shape those extreme deliveries weren't really a risk.

The Coaches then had the players do the same drill without pads, to guide them to play out in front and not create the bat-pad catches that come from using techniques which work well in conditions where the ball turns less sharply.

To develop composure and confidence playing under different conditions, practise your skills and your mental approach under as varied conditions as possible. By reducing your uncertainty about various types of pitches you are once again increasing your chances of success.

Adapt to Bowlers.

Pitches change, but types of bowling change even more often - and with that come mental challenges and opportunities.

Facing fast bowling requires a clear mind, quick reactions, and courage. It's a good test of those Brilliant Basics:

- Trust in your defence and shot making
- Hold your shape
- Have a simple plan
- Look for singles
- Use the pace of the ball.

If fast bowling is troubling you, the first part of the answer is net practice; the second is a Clear Mind (composed, focused, simple, adaptive); and the third, time spent at the crease.

Swing and seam bowlers will aim to deceive you with changes of pace, and movement in the air or off the pitch. As we explored earlier, the key to batting against swing and seam is to reduce the potential for movement. Smart batting is finding tactics that build on your basics, like getting well forward (often supported by batting just out of the crease), shortening your back lift, leaving anything on a length not bowled at the stumps, and attacking (with shape) any overpitched or short delivery.

Mindful Cricketers observe the bowler's actions, grip and field placings. Are they more front on or side on in their action? Is the shine of the ball on one side, or perhaps it's a cross-seam grip? Are field placings set for outswing or shorter of a length?

You can learn a lot by being curious and just observing. Bowlers and captains give away a lot of information about their plans, so these observations can get you a step ahead of the bowler and what they're planning to do.

Spinners come in all styles and techniques, although the two main types are finger spin and wrist spin. Batting Smart against spinners means being aware of the obvious: you'll need to hit the ball, rather than deflect it as you might against the fast bowler. Spinners will be trying variations of turn and flight, all aimed at deceiving you and forcing a false shot. Patience and good judgement, particularly against an accurate spin attack, are the basics for Mindful Cricket, as is being wary when a spinner looks easy to hit, so you avoid overhitting the ball.

The best players of spin bowling combine good defence and agile foot-work with a Play Brave–Play Clever mindset. They enjoy the battle, and have an intent to score, while being very positive and definite in their defence and in leaving the ball. That all comes from practice and mindset.

MINDFUL PRACTICE 3:
Create Partnerships.

One of the most effective ways for the batting team to gain an edge over the bowling team is through partnerships. When two batsmen stay together for a reasonable length of time, they deny the bowlers a wicket and build pressure on the bowlers and fielding captain.

Good players and teams recognise the importance of building partnerships and make it a Brilliant Basic to set team goals while batting. Here's a simple example.

MATCH SCENARIO:

In a weekend 100 over club match, two players came together in the same over in the latter part of the opening session with the score at 75 for 3. The quick loss of two wickets had the bowling team re-energised and expecting more break-throughs in the 30 minutes before the break. Their top quick bowler had taken both wickets and was still getting enough swing and seam to create concern.

The batsmen met mid-pitch and agreed a simple plan: treat the next 30 minutes like the start of an innings, taking it one over at a time and making the bowlers come to them. They'd be alert to quick singles and anything where the bowlers strayed onto the pads. They knew the conditions were quite good, but the two wickets meant the bowlers were probably at their best for a short while.

They blunted the next two overs from the fast bowler, and each scored two singles from the medium pacer bowling from the other end. Early in the third over, the fast bowler dropped short and was put away for a boundary. The next ball was overpitched and driven for another boundary.

At mid-pitch the batsmen noted the bowler was losing shape, so their plan was to stay inside their limitations and if possible, run some quick singles. The next two balls were dropped at their feet and quick singles taken comfortably.

It was the fast bowler's last over and they made it comfortably to the break.

After the break the momentum shifted to the batsmen, with both reaching their half centuries although one player struggled with a leg spinner for a while. To get through that patch they worked the strike and discussed approaches, so the partnership continued into the final overs, when they were dismissed after setting up what became a winning score.

Partnerships are key to holding the tension as a team. Be mindful of momentum shifts and work the strike to capitalise on the partnership.

Watch your teammates' Game Mindset and look for signs when their shape and behaviour shifts. Mid-pitch discussions in between overs help, as can words of encouragement or pointing out they are playing outside their game.

Be attentive to your partner and be a team player. It makes your game stronger.

MINDFUL PRACTICE 4:
Absorb And Apply Pressure.

Cricket is such a tactical game that we could fill a complete book on batting tactics alone. There's a lot to take in, but you'll find an ever-growing set of resources at www.mindfulcricket.com to help improve your personal and team tactics.

What Does "Absorb Pressure" Mean When Batting?

The pressure you feel when batting is more about your reaction to the situation rather than the situation itself. This is a really important point because if it was about the situation, then everyone would experience the same frustrations, impatience, stress and anxiety, which of course they don't.

And be mindful that pressure helps performance, so don't define pressure as when you feel uncomfortable (because that's a good sign), but rather when you are pushed so far into the red zone that timing and judgement are affected.

Mindful Cricket has a host of practices and activities to help you reduce any negative effects of excessive pressure. Here are just a few:

- **Optimistic framing** brings a more optimistic mindset (see Chapter 18)
- **Centred Breathing** calms and quietens the mind
- **Go-To-Plans** bring focus back into the moment, so you don't let the situation get bigger than it needs to be.

And remember, excessive pressure is often created by your own expectations; and that's good, because you can change that by applying some of the practices we discussed in *Defeating Perfectionism and Comparison*.

REFLECTION QUESTIONS

What situations seem to create excessive pressure for you when batting? Is it from a dicey pitch, not scoring, playing and missing, chasing a large score, being physically challenged by fast bowling, or deceived by clever swing or spin? Are there any patterns to when you feel excessive pressure? Does it happen regularly in certain situations, or just occasionally?

Now let's have a look at how pressure builds in matches and what you can do to absorb those pressures and hopefully go on to make the score you want.

Runs are the Pressure Valve.

Every now and then, no matter how good you feel and how well you bat, your best shots just go straight to the fielders. This can build frustration and impatience, which causes many batsmen to needlessly throw away their wickets.

When runs don't come as freely as you might like, the psychological battle can start in your head, long before other people notice. Of course, there's a lot to consider, such as the state of the game, the team score, conditions, quality of the batsmen to come and so on. It's easy to get overwhelmed by the pressure to keep the score moving, but an old-fashioned slog is rarely the answer!

Slow your mind, give the situation some thought, speak with your partner, don't get too far ahead in your thinking.

Teams can and do regularly chase down big scores when they have wickets in hand in the final overs. However, we still see even international players throw their wickets away just because they have been tied down for an over or two in the middle overs.

Cricket matches are won by players who know that the battle takes time and you can't be on top all of the time.

Every aspect of Mindful Cricket plays a part in helping you to absorb and hopefully enjoy the pressures that might have previously caused self-doubt and anxiety.

What Does "Apply Pressure" Mean When Batting?

Batsmen apply pressure in a host of ways to bowlers, fielders and captains, but often they don't realise they are doing it, and therefore fail to fully capitalise on the situation.

Take a moment, breathe and imagine you are batting and want to apply pressure. What are your options? Of course, it depends on the circumstances of the game. Here are ten ways that come readily to mind:

- Take quick singles
- Let good deliveries through to the keeper
- Hit boundaries early in the over
- Chip the ball over fielders
- Use the pace of the ball to your advantage
- Hold your shape confidently in defence
- Show no sign of emotion when you play and miss
- Punish poor deliveries

- Bat out of your crease, or across in front of off stump to upset line and length
- Build a partnership.

Here's a combined Activity and Scenario to test how you think through a game situation.

ACTIVITY: Create Your Scenario.

You've just come off the field after a mediocre bowling and fielding effort. The task is 260 to win from 50 overs. The pitch is good although drying and taking some turn, the outfield slow, and opposition attack has a reputation for accuracy over potency.

Mindful Cricket is being aware of the pressure you build, and how to build pressure in different situations. It's thinking through options, weighing up risk and making decisions.

Remember a key Mindful Cricket principle: Keep it Simple.

What does Keep it Simple mean in this situation? What plan would you suggest for the team and what are the implications for you?

There are many answers, and none guaranteed to succeed, which is why the best option is PDCA with the initial plan suited to team strengths and conditions.

Plan A might be to get away to a solid start, keep wickets intact, and build the foundation for a launch in the second half of the innings. Plan B carries more risk and bigger return by going hard in the first six overs while the field is up, and both openers launching an attack on anything short or overpitched.

Partnerships will probably hold the key to reaching the target, and ideally one of the top-order players becomes established and fills the stable role throughout most of the innings.

Apart from having a clear plan, it's wise to have contingency plans (the "what-ifs") because things will often go better or worse than expected. The what-ifs might include loss of an early wicket, a period of really fast scoring, or perhaps rain delays shorten the chase but increase the runs per over.

Let's approach our scenarios in 10 over blocks and look to win or break even on the momentum in each segment.

10 Over Score: *70 for 3. Well above the run rate, but those three wickets mean an extra fielder is staying in the circle and making it riskier to score. What's your twenty over target and the plan to get there?*

20 Over Score: *100 for 3. The wicket is starting to turn more but you've got two batsmen set. They are working the ball around and the energy has dropped a bit in the field. What's your thirty over target and the plan to get there?*

30 Over Score: *140 for 4. A wicket just fell. You've got good batsmen down to at least 9. What's your forty over target and the plan to get there?*

40 Over Score: *200 for 6. Good run rate but wickets are falling. What's your plan for the next five overs?*

45 Over Score: *235 for 6. The best opposition bowlers will close out the innings. twenty-six needed off five overs. Do you want to take it down to the wire or go harder earlier?*

This scenario is an opportunity to practise your Game Mindset. Don't let the situation be bigger in your mind than it is, slow down when needed, and quieten the noise. Focus one ball at a time.

Key Point Summary.

- Prepare yourself to be confident in seeking out and playing in moments that matter.
- Start smart and Bat Smart in your position.
- Know your shape, trust your shape and know what to do to get your shape back when things get unbalanced and ragged.

- Understand the conditions and what that means for getting the percentages to go in your favour. Observe the bowler's actions, grip and field placings. You can learn a lot by being curious and just observing.
- Be clear about your intent in defence and attack.
- Runs are the pressure valve, so Hold the Tension and trust in your ability to shape the momentum back your way.
- Apply pressure by playing smart cricket. Think through options, weigh up risks and choose the right time.
- Partnerships are key to holding the tension and playing smart as a team.

CHAPTER 14

Bowl Smart.

Bowling is physically different to batting, but the mindset is still about being comfortable and confident to trust your game in moments that matter. Bowlers feel comfortable when they trust their run-up, action and accuracy, while confidence comes from knowing those basics will hold up pressure, and from variations such as pace, swing, and length to outsmart the batsman.

The big question is the same as for the batsman: How can I put myself in the middle of the moments that matter? So, we use the same **four stepping stones** as in the previous Chapter:

- **Smart Bowling Basics** is about building trust in your basics and knowing how to bring them consistently to your game. Those basics include smart first over, line and length and holding shape

- **Adapt to Change** is about mixing up the variations around a solid and reliable stock delivery

- **Create Bowling Partnerships** covers team plans and working together as a unit

- **Absorb And Apply Pressure** includes five "pressure opportunities" to apply pressure to the batsmen.

MINDFUL PRACTICE 1:
Smart Bowling Basics.

Bowling is the most physically demanding of the cricket disciplines, and along with these demands comes the message you've heard repeated many times before: it's doing and trusting your basics in moments that matter.

BASICS 1: Smart First Over.

Smart Bowling starts by being tuned in for your first delivery.

Bowlers who aren't mentally or physically ready tend to make one of two fundamental mistakes on their first delivery: either handing the momentum to the batsman by serving up a juicy half volley or half pitcher, or offering sight of their speciality (outswing, leg spin or whatever) instead of making them play. Does this happen to you?

Being a little nervous is expected, particularly in the first spell of the game. But don't forget how often a wicket falls soon after a bowling change. That makes it doubly important to get the first few deliveries in good areas with rhythm and zip.

> **REFLECTION QUESTIONS**
> *What has happened in your first delivery in recent matches?*
> *Have you practised landing your most reliable stock ball first up in every spell at practice?*
> *What's your percentage accuracy? Don't know? Then how can you improve if you don't measure it in some way?*

Smart Bowling is dropping quickly into a consistent line and length, and that's a skill that comes from practising in the nets and learning from match experiences.

ACTIVITY 1: Smart Start Bowling Drill.

This net activity is intended to reinforce your skill in landing the first delivery of a spell on the intended line and length.

Instructions:

The starting point for Smart Start Bowling is to get into the mindset of bowling spells in the nets rather than just trundling in one delivery after another. To do that, break your bowling into at least three spells at a typical practice session, and create the loosen-up ritual you need to be physically and mentally ready.

At the start of each spell, aim to accurately land your deliveries with the required speed, flight or zip. Make that a specific goal by measuring the landing zone using the grid system we covered in the focusing drills or telling the batsman at the start of each spell you intend to practise dropping quickly into a rhythm and line and length. Have them give you feedback on the first 3-6 deliveries and set yourself a target such as forcing them onto the defensive for those first three deliveries.

· ·

Experiment with short-term goals and rituals to build trust and confidence in starting a spell. The Brilliant Basics Checklist below is a handy resource to help in building the rituals:

BRILLIANT BASICS CHECKLIST – Start Smart Bowling

Here's a Brilliant Basics Checklist for smart starts to your bowling spells:
- Ask the captain to give you an over or more notice
- Loosen and stretch using tested routine
- Mark run-up – and rehearse shape, feel and rhythm through the crease
- Roll over one or two deliveries to a teammate
- Start with a simple plan (make the batsman play your reliable stock ball)
- Focus on rhythm.

BASICS 2: Line and Length.

Smart Bowling is always about the right line and length for your style of bowling and the conditions, so if there is one basic to be brilliant at, this is it!

Research on target sports such as archery and shooting shows that accuracy comes from consistently doing three things:

1. Spotting the middle of the target (not a vague spot)
2. Translating the target into a body feeling
3. Executing the feeling towards the target.

Many baseball pitchers use this approach – spot the target, imagine the feel of the pitch, and then go with the feeling towards the target. What they avoid is over-thinking.

Spot – Rehearse Feel – Just Do It

Did you know that part of your brain is good at planning, and a different part is good at physical execution?

To experiment with this, pick up a ball and choose a target like a bin or a box to lob the ball into. Weigh up the throw you'll need. Take a moment to rehearse the feel of the throw, then just execute that feeling without any further thinking.

Did you get the sense of trusting the "auto-pilot" to just do it, or could you feel yourself still hanging onto control?

If you've ever hit a poor golf shot, you know exactly what I mean by hanging onto control. Instead of choosing the club, rehearsing and then executing smoothly, you hit an awful shot that is so bad you could have done better one-handed while hopping! What happened?

Most likely you were still planning and trying to "think" the ball to the target instead of trusting your own instincts. All the wrong muscles would have been tight (grip, shoulders, legs), whereas by translating the target into "feel" (i.e. a practice swing/imagery) you create rhythm and timing.

Watch a basketballer free throw: Spot, Rehearse Feel, Do It.

The message for cricket? Bowling line and length is about being clever in choosing your target area, and then in translating that into what you want it to feel like in your body.

ACTIVITY 2: Line and Length Test.

From time to time give yourself a real challenge by measuring your ability to hit the target areas more and more accurately.

. . . .

Instruction:
Mark three pitch areas and work with a bowling partner to see who can hit the nominated spot most often while bowling to a batsman. What score will you get?

. . . .

Can you imagine a goal kicker in rugby not practising kicking and measuring accuracy? Any tennis player of reasonable standard will know their first and second serve percentages. For some reason, cricket is still way behind other sports in these very basic measures.

Reminder: Increasing your awareness of "body feel" towards the target will give you more control over the delivery under pressure.

BASICS 3: Hold your Bowling Shape.

Remember the examples of players in snooker, tennis and golf relentlessly drilling their individual "shape" so it holds up under pressure? Shape for bowlers is even more dynamic and more individual than for batsmen. For example, I occasionally see a batsman on television and mistake one player for another, but I instantly recognise the bowlers by their run-up, delivery and follow through.

Bowling Shape is very individual, and very much about body feel and rhythm. It's the feeling of moving seamlessly through your action and follow through. It's having your own triggers, such as the twist of the hips for a spinner, flick of the wrist for the seamer, or pulling down the non-bowling arm in the fast bowler.

Lose shape and you lose pace, control and zip. Watch bowlers closely to see what happens when they lose their shape. Some overstride or stumble in their run-ups, some fall away in their action, and others lose momentum by losing energy in their follow through.

This is where a good coach (and video feedback) will help you to relentlessly work on the cues to your ideal shape as a bowler. These are your Brilliant Basics and will be as much about feel as a plan or list.

Three Activities to Build Confidence in Your Bowling Shape.

To build confidence in your Bowling Shape, there are three basics and an order to approach them. This set of activities provides an overview of each.

· ·

Instructions:

Try these three activities to build awareness and confidence in your Bowling Shape.

ACTIVITY 1: Build Trust in your Delivery Stride

Long jumpers build trust by finding the ideal pace and rhythm for their final two or three strides and the jump. They do this before measuring and locking in a run-up. For some reason cricketers do the exact opposite. To learn about your shape means getting the feel of your final strides and the delivery itself. Common sense says that's best done without a long run-up so that your full attention is on the feel of the action and follow through. Once that's clear, then work your way back to a full run. Give it a try and you'll get more in touch with what your shape feels like than just pounding away off your full run.

ACTIVITY 2: Build Trust in Your Approach to the Wicket

Know the rhythm and feel of your run-up: *length, strides, pace, body position and entry into the action*. Know why you run-up. It has only one purpose: to be in position to deliver the ball.

Get comfortable and confident with your run-up and then learn to adapt when bowling with or into a strong wind. Again, it's about the final few steps. Everything else is just for momentum.

ACTIVITY 3: Always Follow Through

I asked a professional golfer what most often goes wrong with an amateur's swing, and the surprising reply was "follow-through." Further conversation confirmed the follow-through is your commitment to the action. Without it you are slowing down or not fully completing the delivery, or in the golfer's case, the shot. When Nathan Lyon speaks of "bowling over the top" he's giving clues to what shape means for him and how delivery and follow-through are seamless.

· ·

Mindful Cricket is knowing your bowling shape and what to do to get your shape back when things get unbalanced and ragged.

Do you know what to do to get your shape back when things are unbalanced and ragged?

MINDFUL PRACTICE 2: Adapt to Change.

Amongst the most absorbing aspects of cricket are the subtle variations from bowlers of every style. However, this also presents a dilemma of how much to experiment with, and vary the deliveries.

Of course, all bowlers have the option of varying line, length and pace. Fast bowlers have bouncers and yorkers, medium pacers play with swing and seam, and spinners feast on a banquet of flight and spin options including wrong-uns, doosras, arm balls and flippers.

Most of the top international bowlers I've spoken with believe subtle variations are best because of accuracy and being less obvious to the batsman. They also point to the natural variation of a cricket ball with a seam bouncing off a hard surface.

With the possible exception of express pace, bowling usually requires more deception than blasting out a batsman - another reason that tactics and strategies are as important to master as the technical skills.

Trust Your Stock Ball.

Subtle variations are most effective when built on the solid foundation of a good stock ball (or two) which is bowled accurately without leaking unnecessary runs.

A stock ball for quick bowlers is often just short of a length, targeting the top of off stump; for spinners it's a slightly flat delivery turning into a line near off stump; and for medium pacers a well-pitched ball in the corridor of uncertainty just outside off stump.

> **REFLECTION QUESTIONS**
> *What is your stock delivery?*
> *Does it serve the purpose of building pressure by containing the batsmen?*
> *How confident are you to deliver it from the first to last delivery of the day?*
> *Do you have a back-up for different conditions?*

Without a good stock delivery, the better batsmen will just sit and wait for the inevitable poor delivery. When that happens, you've lost control of the momentum and it's back to the nets to get the basics in place so you can play clever cricket.

What percentage of dismissals are caused by batting errors as opposed to exceptional deliveries? My guess is at least 75%, which suggests well over half a team will get themselves out each innings.

For bowlers it's reassuring that you can rely on batsmen to get themselves out provided you apply consistent pressure! It also suggests there are plenty of wickets to be had from a good stock ball, rather than relying on something that swings, seams, dips and hits middle halfway up.

Smart and Subtle Variations.

In good bowling conditions there are plenty of variations available to you, so we won't spend too much time on those here. Instead let's consider some creative options when the batsmen are on top and the ball is not moving in the air or off the pitch.

With a solid stock ball as your basic foundation, start working on two subtle changes:

- The first is to experiment with changes in angle by bowling from close into the stumps and then moving out wide. As always, be mindful of holding your shape and adjusting line to suit the angle.
- The second subtle variation is pace, which means varying the pace from slower to quicker deliveries to suit your style of bowling. Be mindful of maintaining rhythm and accuracy so you aren't offering easy runs.

Six Activities for Variations.

Here are a few other ideas to stimulate your thinking about variations to bring into your game:

Medium-Pacers Variation 1: *Deliver three or four deliveries from a metre or so further back than normal while the same batsman is on strike. It will need practice to get the length right, but it has benefits. Bowl your stock ball with the same rhythm and accuracy you normally use. When you have lured the batsman into playing comfortably, begin your run a metre further up, and give them your best swinging or seaming delivery with the same action as used previously. The extra pace and movement from a metre closer will surprise the batsman and give you a great chance of picking up an edge.*

Medium-Pacers Variation 2: *When the ball is swinging, bowl with exactly the same action as your normal delivery but hold the ball with the shine on the wrong side. For example, if your outswinger to a right-hander is working,* *use your outswing action, put the shine on the off-side (as for an inswinger), point the seam as you would for an outswinger, and aim at or just outside off stump. One of three things will happen:*

- *the ball will go straight and perhaps get an inside edge;*
- *the ball will move in and possibly sneak between bat and pad or hit the pads;*
- *the ball will move slightly away, perhaps not as far as the batsman expects.*

In each case, you have increased your chances of taking a wicket with a subtle variation.

Fast Bowlers Variation 1: *The best fast bowlers employ many of the medium pacer's tricks, while also having the weapons of sheer pace and physical intimidation in their bag. First amongst these is the bouncer, which is as much a psychological weapon as a physical one. Here are variations to try - but be mindful not to overuse this weapon:*

- *high bouncer enticing the batsman to hook or cut in the air;*
- *throat high bouncer which requires evasion or playing;*
- *slower bouncer either as a weapon in a limited over game, or to set up for a faster bouncer to follow;*
- *mixing bouncers and yorkers to create poor footwork for lbw or a false shot;*
- *cross seam or mixed seam grip which creates variation in pace and movement off the pitch.*

Fast Bowlers Variation 2: *A slower ball is a valuable weapon when matched by real pace. Use the slower ball after a couple of quick bouncers, or as the first delivery to a new batsman. Observe the batsmen. Look for players who tend to have their weight back or push with hard hands towards the ball. An accurate, well concealed slower ball might produce a chance in front of the wicket.*

Spin Bowlers Variation 1: *Accuracy and deception are essential to a spin bowler. If you can spin the ball, then drop in one that goes straight on, or actually goes the other way (wrong'un, doosra or arm-ball). Practise this* *in the nets, with the emphasis on perfecting the delivery first and worrying about concealing it later. Even if the batsman can pick your wrong 'un, they still have to play it. Consider using it when a new batsman comes to the crease, following a number of stock deliveries, or when you see a batsman with a technique problem to which you may have an answer!*

Spin Bowlers Variation 2: *Take particular notice of how batsmen play your flighted deliveries. Those who leave their crease present an interesting challenge, particularly if they also like to go through with their shots. Let your wicket-keeper know your plan for a stumping down the leg side. If you are able to get the batsman to believe they can pick your flighted deliveries before you bowl them, you are ready to bowl a quicker delivery down leg side (or wide of off) and collect your prize.*

The only limit to variations in bowling is your imagination and ability to bowl them with reasonable accuracy.

Mindful Bowling is thinking about tactics to dismiss each batsman and being patient in setting up your plan.

Batsmen will get themselves out, but you can give them a helping hand with subtle variations which they might not even notice!

MINDFUL PRACTICE 3: Team Bowling.

Consistently restricting batting sides to less than their average requires more than just the usual expectation of bowlers executing their plans and fielders backing up the bowlers. It requires team bowling, which means a shared bowling plan, commitment from the bowlers operating at any time to synchronise their efforts, and support from fielders.

Team Bowling Plans.

Team bowling plans take the conditions into account, while capitalising on strengths and exploiting the style and limitations of the opposition. The questions to answer in a team bowling plan include:

- What are the pitch and ground conditions?
- What do we know about the strengths, limitations and styles of the opposing batsmen (e.g. attacking/defensive)?
- What are the strengths and limitations of each of our bowlers?
- How can we work as a team to apply optimal pressure?

The best international teams bowl as a unit with a clear plan for the innings and for each individual batsman, and the patience to execute it despite the inevitable shifts in momentum.

How effectively does your team bowl to a plan?

Synchronising Efforts.

There is always a bowler operating at the other end. Effective bowling units give thought to what is going on from both ends and act accordingly. For example, if ten runs come from one over, they keep things tight for an over or two; or if a batsman is struggling against a bowler, they keep them on strike.

How often do wickets fall at the opposite end to a bowler who has dried up the runs? Captains use this tactic by tying down an end with an accurate medium pacer or conservative off spinner and using their quick or less accurate spinner at the other.

Mindful Cricket is a team game, and you'll be a stronger player when you are mindful of ways to strengthen the team.

Team bowling also means sharing your ideas about batsmen and encouraging other bowlers to do the same. Find ways to help each other and to build energy by reinforcing teammates' successes and encouraging them when it is not working.

MINDFUL PRACTICE 4: Absorb And Apply Pressure.

The ebb and flow of momentum in a game is a sure sign of how the batting and bowling teams are Absorbing or Applying Pressure.

Throughout the book we've looked at many practices to Absorb And Apply Pressure, and the recent discussion on bowling variation has provided lots of ideas. Here are a few further ideas and reminders to keep building on that momentum.

What Does "Absorb Pressure" Mean When Bowling?

We know pressure is more about mindset than the situation itself, so what sort of situations build pressure on bowlers? I recently posed this question to a Development Squad doing some work on *Absorbing And Applying Pressure.* They agreed on a "top twelve":

- Losing the toss on flat dry pitch
- Ball not swinging from the start
- Not making the batsman play
- Quick singles – particularly with left/right batters
- Fast start – boundaries in opening overs
- Dropped catches
- Protecting a low score
- Poor umpiring decisions
- Batting partnerships
- Momentum all with batting team
- Injuries
- Out of form bowlers.

It's interesting to reflect on what effect mindset has on each of the pressures listed above, and whether preparation and planning might help. For example, losing the toss, poor umpiring and dropped catches happen frequently, so players can't really say it's a surprise when they happen!

REFLECTION QUESTIONS

What situations seem to create excessive pressure for you when bowling?

Are there any from the items listed by the Development Squad above?

Are there patterns to when you feel excessive pressure? Does it happen regularly, or just occasionally?

Absorbing Pressure means applying the Mindful Cricket basics of composure, focus in the moment and simple plans and adapting fast. That will help avoid letting negatives be bigger than they really are; and it will help you work through tough times with optimism and with plans to make something happen.

Two Quick Wickets

No matter the form of the game, two quick wickets are often enough to shift the whole momentum. At 200/2 in a Test Match, things might look grim, but at 200/4 and with two new batsmen at the crease there is the real chance of a collapse, because the batting side have been sitting watching a run feast and are not mentally ready for pressure.

In tough situations, slow it down, restrict the damage and get control of the things which you can control. Go back to your Smart Basics (line and length, stock ball, bowling to the field). Always bring your Game Mindset Basics – composed, focused, simple and adapting. Things will change. It's cricket. Something will always surprise you.

What Does "Apply Pressure" Mean When Bowling?

Look no further than the previous chapter, when we discussed the pressures experienced by batsmen, to see the options you have as a bowler to use your stock ball and variations to apply pressure.

ACTIVITY: Pressure Opportunities.

This activity has five "pressure opportunities" presented by batsmen, to consider and exploit in your bowling plans. Consider each of these and the Reflection Questions.

. . . .

Instructions:

Consider each of the scenarios and work through the Reflection Questions to build your awareness of pressure opportunities.

New Batsmen: Batsmen want to score. They don't want to be on a duck, and the longer they remain with that zero against their name, the more the pressure builds.

- Do you make a point of keeping a player on their duck for as long as possible?
- Can you build more pressure early in the innings with field placings?
- Are you guilty of giving players easy runs early in their innings?

Struggling Against a Bowler: Bowlers will get on top of some batsmen, and of course the Mindful Batsmen will be good at Holding the Tension and working the strike.

- Are you alert to batsmen being uncomfortable with bowlers, including yourself?
- What strategies work best when you do have a batsman in trouble?
- Is it time to change the field to restrict singles?
- What about when you've beaten the bat a few times but not got an edge? Be mindful of this if it happens often, because you are probably bowling a fraction too short.
- Always be asking: "What does the batsman not want?"

Fall of Wickets: Cricket is a game of momentum, so a break in a partnership is often the switch that changes the momentum from one team to the other.

- Partnerships are the key to batting momentum, so when a new player comes in do you keep them on strike?
- How can you use the loss of wickets to pressure the established player?
- How disciplined are you in sticking to your plan when wickets are falling?

Chasing a Total: Run chases always present a dynamic between bat and ball. In short form games this can shift very quickly with just a few dot balls, or a couple of sixes.

- What strengths do you bring to help apply pressure in a run chase?
- How effectively do you adapt your bowling to saving runs versus taking wickets?
- Do you practise bowling one side of the wicket to restrict the batters?
- What are your "go to" deliveries in the final overs?

Milestone Madness: So many batsmen get dismissed after reaching a milestone (e.g. 50 or 100), or near to break in play.

- Have you doubled down on the pressure when batsmen are close to milestones or breaks?
- How can you alert your team to these opportunities?

Key Point Summary.

- Bowlers feel comfortable when they trust their run-up, action and accuracy; while confidence comes from knowing those basics will hold up under pressure, and from variations such as pace, swing, and length to outsmart the batsman.
- Smart Bowling is starting smart and is always about the right line and length for your style of bowling and the conditions, so if there is one basic to be brilliant at, this is it!
- Bowling line and length is about being clever in choosing your target area, and then translating that into what you want it to feel like in your body.
- Mindful Cricketers know their bowling shape, and what to do to get their shape back when things get unbalanced and ragged.
- Subtle variations are most effective when built on the solid foundation of a good stock ball (or two) bowled accurately without leaking unnecessary runs.
- Consistently restricting batting sides requires team bowling through a shared bowling plan, commitment from the bowlers operating at any time to synchronise their efforts, and support from fielders.
- Absorbing Pressure means applying the Mindful Cricket Basics of composure, focus in the moment and simple plans.

CHAPTER 15

Keep And Field Smart.

A capable wicket-keeper and a team of reliable, energetic fielders play a vital role in supporting the captain and bowlers to Absorb and Apply Pressure throughout the innings.

Many of the principles and practices already discussed in Bat Smart and Bowl Smart apply equally to keeping and fielding, so while not repeating those points, it is important to ensure we bring a Game Mindset into the field.

Let's begin with the wicket-keeper and their role in absorbing and applying pressure.

Smart Keepers Apply Pressure.

The keeper, unlike batsmen or bowlers, has a job to do for the whole innings which means facing a unique combination of physical demands and being fully focused for every delivery.

Competent and consistent keepers lift and sustain the efforts of the whole fielding team through their energy and actions. We only need to see the effect of a keeper spilling catches and letting byes through to see what a difference poor keeping makes to everyone's performance.

If you are a keeper, you have at least five essential roles to play over and above your position in the batting order.

ROLE 1: Catcher, Stumper, Stopper.

Your most vital role is catcher, stumper and stopper, because you can make or break the bowlers by capitalising on any chances they create.

Attentive keepers use mindset skills to catch, stump and stop. They mentally rehearse stumpings, use Resets to switch on and switch off, and use soft hands to give as the ball hits the gloves. They break the game down into segments with Short-Term Goals, Hold Their Shape under the pressure of a tight run-out, and Keep It Simple.

Have you seen how a good keeper Owns Their Space? How they create a sense of order and composure around them? Think about the little rituals and disciplines that send a signal to your team and set a standard. Are you disciplined in your positioning and set-up for each delivery, and neat and tidy in the way you take the ball and send it back to the bowler?

ROLE 2: Leader of the Fielding Effort.

The wicket-keeper is the centrepiece of the fielding effort, handling the ball more often than any other player and getting more catches and run out opportunities.

Standing behind the stumps also puts you in the ideal position to coordinate the fielding effort, including positioning the slips, helping the captain align fielders, directing run-out opportunities, calling for any high catches near the wicket, demanding and encouraging a high standard of throwing, and recognising fielding efforts. All these actions provide leadership in the field.

ROLE 3: Adviser to the Bowlers.

From the position behind the stumps, you see just about everything the batsman sees and are in a great position to spot weaknesses in a batsman's technique. You'll also know how each bowler is performing by the feel of the ball hitting the gloves.

Talk with the bowlers and help them to find strategies to remove a particular batsman. If you see a batsman is susceptible to a type of delivery or is getting frustrated, tell the bowler.

Applaud good deliveries and offer encouragement, because it pressures the batsman and builds your connection with the bowlers. All bowlers appreciate having their good deliveries recognised, and the extra pressure this exerts on the batsman is all part of the game.

ROLE 4: Confidant to the Captain.

Captaining a cricket team is a challenging task and the captain, like any leader, needs reliable sources of information to make the best decisions.

The keeper is one of the most reliable sources of information for most captains because they are in the best position to judge what is happening in the battle between bat and ball. They notice when a bowler is losing energy or becoming a little inaccurate - often a long time before it becomes obvious to players in the slips or at mid-off.

Establishing a trusted relationship with your captain will bring you more responsibility and enjoyment and go a long way towards creating an energetic and reliable bowling and fielding unit.

ROLE 5: Appealing and Chatting.

The keeper and the bowler are the two most important players involved in appealing for leg before wicket and catches behind the wicket. An enthusiastic appeal from these two players seems to increase the chances of a positive umpiring decision.

Umpires are not automatically influenced by the appealing skills of players, but the pressure to award the wicket seems greater when the bowler and keeper both appear totally convinced.

As a keeper, you'll be expected to sustain the "chatter" in the field, and possibly towards the batsmen. What's your thinking about constantly chatting with, or about, the batsmen in between deliveries, as a way of trying to distract their concentration?

Having been on the receiving end of some funny and not so funny chat from keepers, I think there's a line somewhere in the middle where a keeper applies pressure but does it with respect. India's Rishabh Pant probably found that middle line in a Test against Australia where he chatted to Australian Captain and Keeper Tim Paine and offered to look after his children so he could enjoy an evening out with his wife. Clever, funny and no doubt distracting!

How Do We Rate A Keeper?

A wicket-keeper doing their job well is often not noticed and can be taken for granted until something goes wrong. This means the value of a keeper to a team may be underrated by players, so it is important for the keeper to be proficient at assessing their own performance.

Learning to do this to the point where it becomes a habit inevitably helps to sustain and lift performance standards, which in turn has a positive effect on the whole team's effort.

My suggestion to most keepers is to create their own Brilliant Basics Checklist to use as a debriefing tool to review their performance. Within that checklist be sure to include the Mindful Practices associated with composure, focusing in the moment, keeping it simple and adapting fast, because these apply as much to keeping as to any other activity.

ACTIVITY: Create a Brilliant Basics Checklist for Keeping.

This activity is recommended for wicket-keepers to create a template for use when preparing for and debriefing match performances.

Instruction:

Make a list of the keeping activities and actions you feel are most important in preparing for a match and in the match itself.

For example, your list might include pre-game routines, and in-the-game activities such as footwork, watching the ball, staying down to spinners, focusing in the moment, encouraging the fielders, maintaining composure and catching technique.

Use your list as a Brilliant Basics Checklist in preparing for matches and when debriefing your performance. For the debrief choose a rating scale such as points out of ten, where a rating of one means very poor and ten means excellent.

Smart Fielding Applies Pressure.

Alert, enthusiastic and committed fielding applies pressure, and can make even an average bowling team look very good.

A mindful approach is vital to fielding because of the need to be clear and alert every delivery.

> **REFLECTION QUESTIONS**
>
> *What mindset and attitude do you bring to your fielding?*
>
> *Do you focus in the moment and treat it as enjoyable and a challenge?*
>
> *Do you just go through the motions, often distracted, and treat it as something that must be done?*

Mindful Cricket is enjoying fielding and setting high standards across the whole innings and in circumstances that can be unpredictable and high pressure.

When fielding is enjoyable, concentration can seem effortless. Think about the difference between watching an interesting movie and a boring documentary. There is no effort involved in concentrating on something interesting, while your mind constantly drifts away from things that are boring.

Mindset Matters.

"Fielding smarts" are a combination of what you've learned from batting and bowling plus the technical skills. To be a proficient fielder in a range of positions requires well-developed skills such as fielding ground balls, taking catches, and throwing, all supported by agility, judgement and coordination.

Fielding, like all skills, needs to be practised regularly with a mix of basic skills training and simulation of match conditions. Of course, it is easier to set up practice drills aimed at learning and developing skills, than it is to simulate actual match conditions. For example, in a match you may field for three hours before getting one sharp chance to take a catch. This difference between match and practice conditions can be overcome to some extent by including drills where you only get one chance to take a catch, interspersed with long periods of ground fielding (see the High Catch Activity later in the chapter).

The key to fielding concentration is to relax between deliveries and then to call up concentration when needed. Like batting, this requires a ritual or routine using some form of 1-2-3 Reset.

Fielding can also be made more enjoyable by simple visualisation and mental rehearsal skills. While you are in the field, every few minutes imagine that a catch has been hit your way; see yourself taking the catch and pay particular attention to the feeling of taking a catch. This simple technique, which players have used instinctively for years, can help you to react in the way that you need to when a chance does come your way.

The High Catch.

How often do you hear a team-mate say, "If I get a catch, I hope it's a reflex one"?

Players often prefer catches which don't allow them time to think about it. It is questionable whether statistics show they actually catch a higher percentage of the reflex catches; however, it is not a good feeling to "sit underneath" a skied ball and then drop it. Everyone is watching, and as with a short putt in golf, you know you shouldn't miss it, so that "avoid failure" mindset is always a risk.

High catching requires a sound, comfortable and reliable technique and a well-practised mental approach.

Perhaps the greatest problem with high catching is that players often don't use the same thought process when catching balls at training as they do in a match. If you drop a catch at practice, it doesn't really matter because your coach will usually hit another one. The lack of pressure can cause players to be less concerned about dropping the catch and they are more likely to be relaxed, which paradoxically is exactly the way that they need to be in order to catch the high ball. In a match, however, the focus can shift to not wanting to drop the ball, which means tighter muscles, "harder hands" and consequently less chance of catching the ball.

ACTIVITY: Develop a High Catch Mindset.

This simple but practical drill is designed to help you to build confidence and capability in taking high catches.

Instruction:

Work with your coach or teammates on an oval to practise the mindset which goes with catching a high ball.

1. Begin by thinking about the routine that you want to go through once you have sighted the ball. This routine needs to be very simple and involve nothing more than positioning yourself and your hands, watching the ball and anticipating the feeling of taking a soft catch.

2. Make this your Brilliant Basics Checklist and be sure to build in composure, focus and keeping it simple. Above all, go with the attitude of enjoying the challenge.

3. Now work on different types of catches and mix it up so your routine becomes increasingly more reliable. Many coaches weave a high catch competition into training, which means everyone comes out a few times in the session and gets one catch. It's a good way to simulate the game situation.

Fielding Smart in Your Position.

Each position has its own demands, so we should briefly cover them to make sure this is a part of your Game Mindset preparation.

Slips and Gully

If you are fielding in slips and gully, you can expect more catches and less ground fielding than any other fielders in the team. You are a vital part of the team but may contribute nothing to the game for long periods of time. This can be particularly the case for the first slip.

Good slip and gully fieldsmen take the predictable catches as well as the ones that come out of the blue. This comes from well-practised reflexes, supported by good concentration and self-confidence.

To switch on concentration, try using a cue from the bowler's run-up to begin and then switch off again as soon as it is clear that you have no role to play in fielding the ball (including backing up).

Close to the Wicket

These roles aren't usually the most popular position as they can be dangerous because of full-blooded shots. If you have ever fielded at short leg, you will know you can't really see what the ball is doing, and it can also be physically uncomfortable to crouch in this position for long periods of time.

To succeed as a close-in fielder requires excellent concentration skills because, as for the slips and gully fielders, the chances will be few and far between. It can also be tempting to jump or look away whenever the batsman shapes to play a shot, but easy catches can be missed if you do this. This makes courage and judgement important components of the close-in fielder's psychological make-up. Perhaps this explains why many good close fielders have also been opening batsmen who regularly face physical danger as part of their day-to-day trade.

Outfielding

Outfield positions include fine leg and deep third man, together with many forward-of-the-wicket positions.

The role of the outfielder varies depending upon the size of the ground. On a small ground the main emphasis can be on cutting off boundaries and trying to reduce well-hit shots to singles. On larger grounds, where it is more difficult for batsmen to hit boundaries, the key is to reduce the runs by getting to the ball quickly.

As always, concentration is important, as are anticipation, good running speed and a strong throwing arm. For example, if when fielding at deep mid-wicket you can quickly pick up the line that the ball is taking, move speedily to gather the ball, and dispose of it quickly and accurately with a strong throw, then runs can be saved and run-outs created.

The Infielder

The infield includes cover, square leg, point and mid-wicket, mid-on and mid-off. These are where most fielders are positioned - and there are a variety of roles to perform.

As an infielder, be alert and aware of the batsman's intentions. Move in with the bowler and be ready to pounce on the ball if it is hit in your direction and look to create run out opportunities. When the ball is hit to the other side of the wicket you also have an important role to play in backing up the throws that come into the wicket. Good backing-up is a feature of good fielding sides, as it requires concentration and discipline.

Set the Team Standards.

Wicket-keeping and fielding are two of the least rewarded aspects of the game. However, the standards set behind the stumps and in the field often determine just how successful your team will be. These standards are as much a function of mindset as they are of physical skills. With concentration, backed up by well-practised skills, an ordinary bowling attack can be made to look quite special.

Setting and sustaining high standards in the field is fundamental to Mindful Cricket.

Is there scope for you to improve in this area?

Key Point Summary.

- The wicket-keeper and a team of reliable, energetic fielders play a vital role in supporting the captain and bowlers to Absorb and Apply Pressure.
- Unlike batsmen or bowlers, the keeper has a job to do for the whole innings, which means they face a unique combination of physical demands and the imperative to be fully focused for every delivery.
- As wicket-keeper you are the centrepiece of the fielding effort, handling the ball more often than any other player and getting more catches and run-out opportunities.
- From the position behind the stumps you see just about everything the batsman sees and are in a great position to spot weaknesses in a batsman's technique.
- Establish a trusted relationship with your captain.
- Alert, enthusiastic and committed fielding applies pressure, and can make even an average bowling team look very good.
- The key to good concentration while fielding is to relax between deliveries and then to call up concentration when needed. As with batting, it will help to develop a ritual or routine using some form of 1-2-3 Reset.
- Wicket-keeping and fielding are two of the least rewarded aspects of the game. However, the standards set behind the stumps and in the field often determine just how successful your team will be.

Pillar 4.
Play Better

Learn and Develop.

Play Better means having a continual belief in your ability to learn and adapt in a fast-changing environment, and the self-discipline to set up to be your best when the opportunity arises.

When writing this book, I wondered whether to place the principle of Adapt Fast in this section. However, the mindset of PDCA Learning Loops is so important as a core principle that it had to be a part of Clear Mind.

Accordingly, Play Better still rests heavily on that principle and the related practices, while bringing together three other principles which feature strongly in the Game Mindset of players who do well over long periods of time:

- Growth Mindset
- Be Game Ready, and
- Bring Optimism.

The first, Growth Mindset, is such an important topic. It is about believing that talent and ability aren't fixed, and therefore we can learn and get better by putting in the effort. Here we explore three strategies commonly employed by high performers to build and capitalise on Growth Mindset:

- taking a strengths first approach,
- finding and accepting feedback, and
- taking care of yourself.

Many people think we have either a Growth Mindset or a Fixed Mindset all the time. You'll learn that is not the case; there will be times where you bring a Growth Mindset and other times where your mindset is definitely fixed.

The second principle, Be Game Ready, is about raising awareness of what makes you think and feel at your best, and the daily habits that consistently create the conditions for that to happen. You can then use those insights to create your pre-game and pre-performance routines and rituals.

Perhaps the most compelling insight here is:

The way you organise and conduct yourself during the week has a direct and lasting impact on the way you play on the cricket field.

This means if you want to perform more consistently near your best on the cricket field, then look to build consistency into your daily habits or rituals, because very few players can be disorganised all week and then bat or bowl in a disciplined way when the match begins.

This section closes out with the third principle, Bring Optimism, which highlights how we see the world differently depending on whether our "mindset filter" is optimistic or pessimistic. You will explore practices designed to develop your optimistic filter to create a way of thinking which reduces anxiety and improves confidence and outcomes.

Play Better is a great reminder that we all have the capability to improve, and we can build that capability through strengthening our mindset and thinking. Let's explore how.

CHAPTER 16

Apply A Growth Mindset.

Growth Mindset is one of those concepts which seem so blindingly obvious that only an academic mind would find it interesting, or of practical value:

Talent and abilities aren't just genetic traits fixed in place. Work hard, learn, and we will improve and be more successful.

It's not really rocket science, is it? And yet this distinction between Growth Mindset and Fixed Mindset, discovered through the research of Stanford University Psychologist Carol Dweck (2008), reveals so much about how to Play Better and why our development as cricketers slows or stops at times.

Cricket is a sport where great players are revered as having God-given talent, and judgements on all others seem to go straight to unchangeable limitations:

He can't make runs on seaming pitches. She can't bowl long spells. She's not tall enough to bowl fast at this level. He just can't play the short ball. Players at Test level don't need coaching. You're either good enough or you're not once you reach this level. She hasn't got the temperament for this. He just isn't smart enough to play clever cricket.

Fixed Mindset. Every statement above has one underpinning belief: players have fixed limits. Perhaps they do, but few come even close to reaching them.

Cultivate a "Not Yet" Attitude.

Growth Mindset is believing in the power of learning and growing. Ironically, it's about failure.

Do you have the curiosity, courage and desire to push out of the comfort zone which protects you with beliefs such as: "I'm just not good at maths, hook shots, bowling into a strong wind, talking to groups, etc?" If that's your mindset, you are thinking in terms of "pass or fail" instead of "not yet."

Listen to cricket commentary and interviews. You rarely hear a Fixed Mindset amongst the top current day players (who are always thinking "not yet"), but you'll often hear it from former players who seem so ready to label players in "pass/fail" terms.

Growth Mindset is optimistic:

He's not yet learned to make runs on seaming pitches. She hasn't yet developed the skills and stamina to bowl long spells. Players at Test level seem to grow and develop faster because they meet the challenges head on. She's working on her temperament and getting better at reading the game.

SELF-ASSESSMENT: What Mindset Do You Bring?

This brief but powerful self-assessment asks you to think about the mindset you bring to challenges and to your own growth and development.

Instructions:

Reflect on the items in the table below. Which of each pair is most like you?

I go towards risks and challenges	<->	*I avoid risks and challenges*
I think about strengths first	<->	*I think about weaknesses first*
I bounce back from setbacks	<->	*I get knocked off track by setbacks*
I'm open to failing and getting feedback	<->	*I don't react well to failure or feedback*
I take care of my body and mind	<->	*I take my body and mind for granted*

Take a Centring Breath and then reflect on what this self-assessment tells you.

Cultivating a "not yet" attitude to cricket and life sets you up to learn and develop rather than being restricted by beliefs that simply aren't true. Not surprisingly, the best coaches create a culture or environment where players feel able and empowered to take the risks needed to go beyond their current limits and learn to play better.

Mindful Practices for Growth.

Many people think we have either a Growth Mindset or a Fixed Mindset all the time. That is not the case. There will be times where you bring a Growth Mindset and other times when a Fixed Mindset emerges. For example, when you are tired or feel overwhelmed, a Fixed Mindset might show through, whereas in the blue zone you might notice Growth Mindset at play.

The key question is whether you can switch on Growth Mindset when it matters to help breakthrough in areas that are holding you back. And the good news is that the research evidence from Carol Dweck and others is super strong: You can develop Growth Mindset.

With that optimistic view in mind, let's explore three strategies I've consistently seen amongst cricketers which highlight why and how Growth Mindset and Fixed Mindset affect development and performance. I have used two edited Mindful Journal reports from players and a challenge to you, so you get a very personal view of the journey to awareness of mindset, acceptance of your role in changing it, and the actions you can take to make positive lasting change.

MINDFUL PRACTICE 1: Strengths First.

This strategy is from the journal of a 16-year-old female wicket-keeper/batsman.

I really got lots of value from learning about Growth Mindset and cricket. We did this topic in school, but it was only when our cricket team did a session with a sport psychologist that I realised my own Fixed Mindset.

Cricket isn't the main sport at school and I'm not very good at netball, basketball or tennis, so it was kinda the last option. The team needed a wicket-keeper, and the coach tried out a few people and amazingly I was the one she chose.

The girls thought it was funny, although they stopped laughing and started criticising when I dropped catches and missed stumpings in matches. I was so embarrassed. I was expecting to drop a catch every ball and would do anything to give the gloves to someone else.

The stuff on Growth Mindset opened my eyes to three things:

First, my whole focus was on weaknesses, even though my coach says I take the ball cleanly and have good footwork. So, my first action was to write down my strengths and start using them.

Second, I was making excuses to get out of practice sessions because I was embarrassed. I needed to face that down.

Third, my thinking was so self-defeating and in the past. I realised I had to stop being my own critic and believe I was getting better every day (which I was!!).

When I debriefed this with my coach we settled on the slogan "Strengths First", which means know my strengths and build on them; and then instead of listening to criticism about weaknesses, I'll improve by working at them.

We've been working on a simple plan each week to build on my strengths and practice areas that are "Not Yet" and it's just been so much better. I've also found the 1-2-3 Reset really helpful to keep me focused in the moment.

To reflect on the value of a "Strength First" approach to your cricket, do the activity below.

ACTIVITY: Creating a Strengths Portfolio.

This activity encourages you to identify and record key strengths in your game. It will be helpful when developing Go-To-Plans, and in building self-confidence.

. . . .

Instructions:

Start by reflecting on the following points:

- People have different strengths, and no one is good at everything
- Our strengths change over time as do our expectations of what a strength means
- Doing things we are good at increases energy and motivation.

Give some thought to the three questions below and jot those thoughts in your journal for ongoing reflection:

1. What strengths do you currently have in cricket?
2. How can you better use and develop these strengths?
3. What strengths do you want to have one year from now?

Finally, allow yourself time to genuinely reflect on the answers in each area, and in particular, what you can do to put strengths first in your thinking.

. . . .

MINDFUL PRACTICE 2:
Find Challenging Feedback.

This second strategy is a challenge to you.

If there is one topic more than any other sitting at the heart of Growth Mindset, it is attitude towards feedback. Without feedback you can't learn. However, challenging feedback (i.e. feedback which challenges the way you think and act) can sting, so it's no wonder many players go out of their way to avoid it.

How do they avoid it? By ignoring it, not taking risks, denying they were really trying, or by being defensive or aggressive towards the person offering the feedback.

Challenging feedback presses emotional buttons. A coach or another player might say your defensive game isn't as good as you thought. Ouch. You might feel the need to defend yourself but pause for a moment because it might help you to learn faster.

Here's an important question: Is it more important to prove how good you are now, or to speed up your development? If it's the latter, then feedback is essential as it might help to improve the way you receive feedback.

ACTIVITY: Get the Most from Feedback – The 3Rs.

This activity introduces a very practical tool to help you to strengthen your ability to effectively receive and process challenging feedback.

Instructions:

Next time you get some challenging feedback, resist the urge to react immediately and instead try **The 3Rs: Receive, Reflect, Respond.**
Here are the steps for each:

Receive the feedback by showing you are open to it. Take a Centring Breath, then show it in your body language, in the way you listen and are curious to learn. In the first few seconds only say, "thank you", then move to the next "R."

Reflect means to pause (breathe) and think about what you've been told, separate the emotion from the message, and take time to choose what is of value to you and your goals. Not all feedback is going to be useful or accurate, so if it's hard to get perspective by yourself, ask a coach or friend to help you reflect.

Respond with action. That might mean asking for more feedback or experimenting with new approaches.

· ·

Mindful Cricket is finding valuable feedback to help reinforce strengths and create ways to learn and improve.

What you do with that feedback is your responsibility, but a key is to seek quality feedback from people you respect. Who comes to mind as someone who will give you "non-sugar-coated" and valuable feedback?

Use the 3Rs whenever you receive feedback, so you get the most value while also encouraging others to continue offering it. And be mindful that positive feedback needs the same 3Rs process so you can sort what's of value from what is just ego massage.

MINDFUL PRACTICE 3: Take Care.

This final strategy is perfectly explained in the brief but compelling journal of an international player:

Credit where credit is due. I was on a fast track to wrecking my career until one of the academy coaches got me to have a chat with the performance psych coach. I was training and competing every minute of every day. I didn't do recovery or any of the mindful stuff because I thought I was tough enough to not need it. Instead, I tried to win everything at training; taking more wickets, hitting the ball further and always being at the front of any runs or gym work.

I started getting physical niggles in my back and hamstring, so I just did more stretching and went through the pain. Then the coaches took me aside and said my teammates thought I wasn't a team player. I told them it wasn't about making friends. I was in this to be the best. If people didn't like it, well, bad luck.

They dropped me, and at the same time I was diagnosed with a stress fracture.

Cut a long story short. The psych helped me extract my head from you know where. I started taking care of myself and showing some care and respect for others. He called it "Take Care." It's why I'm now a successful professional cricketer and not a broken wreck.

The message about self-care is easily forgotten when we are busy and occupied with day-to-day demands.

Mindful Cricket is taking care of yourself.

Remember that it's impossible to sustain high levels of performance without giving attention to "fuelling" your mind and body. Pause now and take the time to reflect on the five items in the checklist in the following activity because they are all about building and sustaining the energy and focus which sit at the centre of mindful cricket.

ACTIVITY: Taking Care of Yourself.

This activity introduces the concept of self-care and provides a basic checklist to reflect on practices.

Instructions:

Consider each of the items below and rate whether it is something you are doing well or there is need to improve. Give yourself a score out of 10.

- **Physical wellbeing** (sleep, nutrition, stretching, hydration)
- **Emotional wellbeing** (rest, relaxation, balance, calmness)

- **Intellectual wellbeing** (learning, stimulation)
- **Relationships** (family, friends, teammates, coaches)
- **Spiritual** (faith, connection).

Be mindful of how you are constructing your week and whether you are taking care of yourself, which means looking after your most important asset. The next chapter has some excellent tips on building good daily habits.

Making the Three Strategies Work for You.

The three strategies for Growth Mindset provide a compelling insight into the difference between Growth and Fixed Mindset, and how development moves through Awareness, Acceptance and then Action.

It starts with the simple phrase "not yet'" and from there you have the skills and resources to build it into your Game Mindset.

Mindful Cricket is about developing the patience and courage to let go of defensiveness and be open to learning and growing.

REFLECTION QUESTIONS

Are you bringing a Growth Mindset to your cricket?

Are you aware of things which push you towards a Fixed Mindset at times (e.g. tiredness, challenging feedback)?

Is there one action you could take to strengthen your Growth Mindset?

What benefits would you hope to gain from doing that?

Key Point Summary.

- Talent and abilities aren't just genetic traits fixed in place.
- Growth Mindset is believing in the power of learning and growing. Ironically, it's about failure. Work hard, learn and you will improve and be more successful.
- Instead of "Pass or Fail", think "Not Yet."

- Strengths First: Focus on strengths not weaknesses, avoid making excuses and challenge the self-defeating thinking which is anchored in the past and doesn't define your future.
- Find Challenging Feedback: Focus on how fast you are developing and not on how good you are. Welcome feedback by using the 3Rs: Receive, Reflect, Respond. It's your choice.
- Take Care: Protect your most important asset. You!

CHAPTER 17

Be Game Ready.

What frame of mind are you in when you arrive at practice and games? They'll be different of course, but both need a clear mind (composed, focused, simple, adaptive), which will always be the foundation for Mindful Cricket. Consider for a moment a deep truth:

The way you organise and conduct yourself during the week has a direct and lasting impact on the way you play on the cricket field.

Want to perform more consistently near your best as a cricketer? Then build consistency into your daily habits or rituals, because very few players can be disorganised and inconsistent all week and then bat or bowl in a disciplined way for hours.

MINDFUL PRACTICE 1:
Build Your Daily Habits.

Players with good daily habits tend to be less externally driven and distracted by pressures and distractions coming at them when working, studying or playing cricket.

Good daily habits in the form of "little rituals'" build a sense of confidence and security, while also laying the foundation for building the all-important pre-game rituals. How? Start by being mindful of what works for you and what doesn't, or more specifically what makes you feel good (blue zone!).

Mindful Cricket means being an astute observer of your physical and mental state.

It's noticing and learning what makes you feel energised and what makes you feel flat. It's understanding the causes of mind drift and how you experience composure, clarity and simplicity.

You can use those insights to create habits that work for you - not rigid, boring disciplines, and or a "magic bullet" from a sporting champion. Use simple rituals and disciplines suited to your individual personality and built into your day, and then into your pre-game pattern.

Four Daily Habits

High performers in all areas of life tend to build a common set of basic daily habits. There are four in particular which have real value for cricketers. As you consider them, keep in mind that this is about building your own unique daily habits and rituals which make you feel, think and perform better.

HABIT 1: Optimal Hydration.

Dehydration is a primary cause of low energy and poor focus, which makes it a great place to start shaping your daily habits by running some experiments to see what effect intake of fluid has on your mental and physical state.

Over 60% of your body weight is water, so not surprisingly every cell, tissue and organ depend on water to operate effectively. Without enough water, waste accumulates, temperature rises, joints stiffen, and tissues are more susceptible to damage. If you are at all dehydrated, there will be no Clear Mind.

ACTIVITY: Test Your Hydration.

. . . .

Instruction:
My business and sport clients often report that just one week of experimenting with how water impacts their mind and body has revealed

that tiredness, slight headaches and struggling with focus in the afternoon are resolved by better hydration.

. . . .

The amount of water you need depends on lots of things – age, exercise, humidity, body weight, health and so on - so it's best to experiment. Why not try that for a week and see what you observe and learn?

HABIT 2: Stretch, Loosen and Recover

A daily ritual of stretching is close to a "must do" for any high performer. Whether that means yoga, foam rollers or general stretching, it is all about what makes you feel and perform at your best. Add to that whatever helps you to recover from training or stress, such as sauna, showers, a walk on the beach or in nature etc, and you are taking care of your greatest asset - you!

These daily rituals also set the foundation for your pre-game warm-up, which is essential for mental and physical preparation. Game focus won't suddenly happen at the moment that you begin to bat or bowl — you need to create the opportunity for it to happen. A thorough, systematic warm-up underpinned by good hydration will help to achieve this.

ACTIVITY: Test Your Stretch, Loosen and Recover Rituals.

. . . .

Instruction:
Reflect on the things you currently do that help you to stretch and loosen so you can feel and perform at your best. Then look at the activities that help you to recover from training and the daily stresses of life.

Look at how you structure your days and consider whether there are little rituals you can build into preparation and recovery to trigger the blue zone, which is pivotal to creating and sustaining your Game Mindset.

. . . .

HABIT 3: Pacing For Pressure.

What's your natural pace or cadence? Do you like to do things fast, or is your drumbeat slower and more methodical? What happens to your pace and thinking when you're under pressure?

As pressure builds, most people notice three things happening:

1. **Thoughts and actions speed up** - they move faster, jump from one thing to another and react quickly;
2. **Noise increases in their mind** - more thoughts, more issues to handle, more options to consider;
3. **Focus shifts to the consequences** - what will happen in the future, what if?

Clever cricket is doing the opposite of these three practices. Instead of speeding up, slow it down; instead of adding to the noise, quieten it down; and instead of allowing mind drift towards the consequences, focus on one ball at a time.

ACTIVITY: Test Your Pacing For Pressure.

How can you train yourself to control the pace when things seem to be speeding up? Simple. Capture the countless opportunities every day to slow it down, quieten it down, and focus on one step at a time. Consider how you might build little rituals based on the Mindful Cricket practices we've been covering, such as Centred Breathing, 1-2-3 Reset and Letting Go.

Here are a few reminders and ideas to guide you on these three Brilliant Basics:

Slow it down: *Build in short pauses between activities in your day, and in your reaction to distractions. For example, instead of grabbing for your device when you leave a meeting or as soon as it pings, pause for a moment, take a Centring Breath and then respond as you choose to.*

Quieten the Noise: *Be mindful of when your thoughts are becoming jumbled or negative. Look for times when you are making a situation bigger than it needs to be. That might be when you are stuck in a traffic jam or frustrated by someone's behaviour. Take an intentional breath, and as you breathe reframe the situation more optimistically. Take every opportunity in these day-to-day moments to quieten the noise. It will pay big dividends in your cricket.*

Ball-By-Ball: *Catch yourself whenever you are trying to do two things at once or worrying about the future instead of focusing on the now. Be deliberate in focusing on one thing. Give it your attention, whether it's a conversation, study or cleaning your home. The more you practise compartmentalising, so you focus on one thing at a time, the better you'll do under pressure.*

HABIT 4: Set Up to Suit Yourself.

Do you waste time or energy in your day-to-day life because of lack of clear priorities or distractions? What causes these lapses?

The answer might lie in the structure of your day and the environment you create around yourself:

How do you currently structure your day?
What sort of waking, rest and sleep routines work best for you?
What set-up of tools and physical layout suit you?

For example, I travel every week, which means well over 100 plane flights a year and plenty of different environments. Accordingly, I have a range of simple habits, rituals and equipment to help me perform and relax anywhere, anytime. This includes songs on my smartphone, earphones and a backpack with items like keys, pens, laptop and snacks with easy access. I have Evernote on my phone and laptop to keep important information, a Kindle to read novels and business books, and travel lists to ensure minimal time and maximum accuracy in packing. I also have some simple rituals, like a pre-sleep process which helps me transition from work thinking into a state where I get that all-important 7-8 hours' sleep.

When we look at your pre-game rituals in a moment, it's unlikely they'll be any more effective than the way you structure your day or create the environment around you.

ACTIVITY: Test Your Set Up.

Instruction:
Reflect on the way you organise your day, and the tools and resources you use to bring comfort and focus.

Are there opportunities to subtly improve your waking, rest and sleep routines?

What set-up of tools and physical layout of your work or study spaces can be redesigned to suit you better?

Without the right set up it will be difficult to bring energy to your cricket and other important areas of your life.

MINDFUL PRACTICE 2:
Create Your Pre-Game Routine and Rituals.

Mindful Cricket is about performing consistently, and one of the most reliable ways to create consistency is good preparation.
Pre-game routines and rituals will help you to do that and they will mostly be an extension of your daily habits, so we will go straight into an activity built on four steps to help you design and refine your pre-game rituals.

ACTIVITY: Design Your Game Readiness Plan.

This activity guides you through four steps to design a pre-game routine with rituals that get you into the optimal physical and mental shape. Visit www.mindfulcricket.com for guidance on this activity.

. . . .

Instructions:

The following four steps build on the awareness you gained from exploring the zone, and from experimenting with daily habits. The steps are:

1. **Know What Game Ready Means**
2. **Assemble the Pieces**
3. **Draft Your Game Readiness Plan**
4. **PDCA Your Plan.**

Take time to get your Game Readiness Plan into a shape that works best for you across all the conditions where you play the game.

STEP 1: Know What "Game-Ready" Means

Think about the matches coming up and ask yourself these questions: If I was totally ready to perform at my best...

- mentally – what would I be thinking?
- emotionally – how would I be feeling?
- physically – what shape would I be in?
- environmentally – what set-up would I create?

Jot down your thoughts on each of these so you can sort them and reflect on them now and in the future as you continue to fine-tune your rituals. Take into account what you need for batting, bowling and keeping.

STEP 2: Assemble the Pieces

Think back over the past season to matches when you felt most comfortable and in control of your game from the start:

What did you do to create the environment where you were mentally, physically and emotionally set up to succeed?

Here are some prompts to stimulate your thinking:
- What were your habits and rituals in the week leading up to the game?
- How did you practise?
- Did you think a lot or little about the game?
- What helped you to be physically energised?
- What attitude did you bring?
- What warm-up and final preparation did you do?
- How did you deal with distractions or "noise"?

Use the insights to identify what seems to be essential to set you up for your blue zone. Aim to keep it as simple as possible and don't be concerned if you aren't sure, because this is a starting point to build on.

This is where your attention to daily habits and rituals is likely to offer really useful insights.

STEP 3: Draft Your Game-Readiness Plan

Start a week out from the game and draft a plan describing the behaviours and set-up you want to include in your Pre-Game Rituals. The table below shows a structure and examples:

WHEN	WHAT AND HOW
Weekly	Set goals, priorities and timelines for the week, including reviewing opposition and likely conditions, and defining key themes
Daily	Maintain daily hydration, stretching, sleeping and centring practices
Day Before	Gather gear, define simple game plan, do 20 minutes mental practice
Morning	Meal, stretch, visualise and do some reflex catches
Warm-Ups	Be in first group, dynamic stretch, work up to 90% pace, have brief throw downs
In Game	Equipment ready, Use Go-To-Plan

STEP 4: PDCA Your Plan

These questions are framed around PDCA, and will help you to refine your Game Readiness Plan:

- **Plan:** When and how are you going to begin using the plan?
- **Do:** Give it a go, because it's only as good as the value you get from doing it
- **Check:** Reflect on what worked, what didn't work and what needs changing
- **Adapt:** Adjust the plan and PDCA again.

The main intent of PDCA is to build a Learning Loop so you continuously improve from one experience to the next, so it makes sense to do the Check after a match, to reflect on what worked and what might be improved.

MINDFUL CRICKET TOOL:
Brilliant Basics Batting Readiness Checklist.

Here's an example of a Brilliant Basics Readiness Checklist for batting, which may be helpful as you run the PDCA Loop over your batting plans:

Get all gear together
Stretch and loosen up
Twenty throwdowns in nets or on oval
Refine and commit to simple game plan
Pad up slow
Place all gear ready to move
Observe game – mind frame positive
Wicket falls – go at my pace
On oval – loosen and adjust
Take block, check field
1-2-3 Set - ready

Use the Brilliant Basics Checklists to the extent that they help you find your blue zone. Don't overdo it. Just feed this into your thinking about what works best for you.

Key Point Summary.

- The way you organise and conduct yourself during the week has a direct and lasting impact on the way you play on the cricket field.
- Good daily habits in the form of "little rituals" build a sense of confidence and security, while also laying the foundation for building the all-important pre-game rituals.
- Dehydration is a primary cause of low energy and poor focus, which makes it a great place to start shaping your daily habits.
- Daily rituals of stretching, loosening and recovery help build and sustain energy; and they set the foundation for your pre-game warm-up, which is essential for mental and physical preparation.
- Capture the countless opportunities every day to slow down, quieten down, and focus one step at a time.
- Give attention to how you structure your day and to creating the environment around you that serves you best.
- Mindful Cricket is about performing consistently, and one of the most reliable ways to create consistency is good preparation.
- Create and continually refine your pre-game routines and rituals to help you to be in the optimal mental and physical state to perform.

CHAPTER 18

Bring Optimism.

As I walked past two players waiting their turn to bat, I paused and listened:

I never play well when we bat first. Why did we bat first? This pitch is hopeless. You can't make runs out there.

This is an extreme example, I'll admit, but it is a perfect illustration of minds focused towards difficulties, barriers and weaknesses. Imagine if the bowlers had the same approach. Their conversation might go something like:

I never bowl well into the wind. I can't bowl to left-handers. Why am I bowling from this end? If I get the edge, they'll probably drop the ball anyway.

We See Life Through a Filter.

Just as a camera takes different pictures depending on the filter over the lens, we see the world differently depending on the filters we use.

The players in the example above seem to have a strong "pessimistic filter", and chances are they'll be less confident, more stressed, and lower performing than if they had chosen an "optimistic filter".

This distinction between optimism and pessimism is one of the strongest predictors of success in study, career and sport. However, we're not talking about wishful thinking or head-in-the-sand positive thinking. The key is how you interpret a situation.

Spiral or Springboard?

A player with an optimistic filter believes there are possibilities, while the player with the pessimistic filter does not. That's mindset. It's focusing on what you have, not what you don't have. It's looking for a way forward rather than wallowing in self-pity.

> *It's being mindful to avoid the negative pessimistic spiral which describes one of the golden rules of sport psychology:*
>
> *Our own mistakes and the opponent's good luck have much less impact on whether we achieve our goals than what we do immediately after it happens.*

Watch a good opening batsman cope with a seaming pitch by playing one ball at a time while not letting a dropped catch, multiple play-and-misses or extravagant movement off the pitch affect their focus and shape on the next delivery. They're in the moment, not in the past or too far into the future. They're making the most of the situation by seeing possibilities.

Contrast that to the frustrated bowler losing control of line and length and taking the pressure off the batsman. They're thinking in the past, feeling sorry for themselves, blaming someone or cursing their bad luck.

Are the following examples familiar from your experience with cricket and cricketers?

PESSIMISTIC MINDSET	OPTIMISTIC MINDSET
Stresses over a poor shot	Resets to play the next ball well
Assumes losing the toss is a disaster	Has a plan to put pressure on opponents
Expects bad things to happen	Keeps working to make good things happen
Ignores little things that go well	Seeks small victories
Blames the umpire	Accepts and moves on
Shows negative reactions to opponents	Projects positive body language
Remembers bad shots or deliveries	Remembers good shots or deliveries
Unwilling to try new things	Willing to try new things

REFLECTION QUESTIONS

Which of these statements best describes you?

- *I usually do well in challenging circumstances*
- *I usually don't do well in challenging circumstances*
- *I expect good things to happen*
- *I expect bad things to happen.*

Whatever your answer, there is value in strengthening your ability to frame situations with an optimistic mindset.

Optimism Can Be Developed.

The good news is an optimistic frame of mind can be learned and strengthened by applying simple mindful tools to cricket challenges. Many schools around the world include optimism training in their curriculum because these are skills which can be learned.

As with any mindful approach, the starting point is awareness, which means being alert to the way you frame situations as they arise. For example, while writing this section of the book I have just been interrupted by a call from a business client with some news which disrupts our plans for the next few weeks. I've caught myself putting on the pessimistic filter and making this bigger and more negative than it really is. It's a nice reminder of how easily we slip into the pessimistic frame of mind, but also how effective the following simple activities and tools can be for generating a more optimistic way of thinking.

Here are three basic activities and tools to use when you want to bring optimism:

- Change your filter
- Choose optimistic language
- Be grateful.

ACTIVITY 1: Change Your Filter.

Be aware of and take responsibility for how you filter or frame situations. This activity is an obvious and effective way to strengthen your optimistic mindset by being aware when you experience a "mind drift" towards the pessimistic.

· ·

Instructions:

See if you can notice when uncomfortable emotions such as frustration, anger or disappointment are creeping into your game and affecting your mindset. This certainly doesn't mean obsessing over every thought, but just pausing when you notice, and doing four things:

1. **Note what you are doing - e.g. bowling to a batsman who is on top.**
2. **Describe the feeling - e.g. becoming frustrated.**
3. **See how your thinking is changing - e.g. getting down on yourself and losing shape.**
4. **Bring your thinking back to being more optimistic - e.g. do a 1-2-3 Reset, or a Go-to-Plan.**

For example, when bowling you might notice a feeling of tightening up and starting to worry about stemming the flow of runs. Instead of reinforcing the thoughts just note the feeling, take a Centring Breath, and refocus on Applying Pressure back to the batsman.

· ·

When coaching a group of bowlers in this activity, I asked what thoughts were helpful when the batsmen were on top. They created a shared list which included:

· Let's take it one ball at a time
· The ball's not swinging but we can still use some changes of pace
· Keep working, the edge will come
· Keep the rhythm.

We talked about their experience with pessimistic filtering and how it affected their thinking and execution. As part of the discussion I asked what signals in the game they give power to - the positive signs or the negatives? Most admitted they gave the negatives too much power. There's awareness for all of us in that insight.

ACTIVITY 2: Choose Optimistic Language.

This activity helps to create awareness of the impact on mindset and performance of the words or phrases we use in thinking or speaking.

Instructions:
Words like "never", "can't" and "yes but" can be self-defeating and set up a pessimistic filter which makes you sound and feel less powerful and able to find possibilities.

- What language do you use when discussing an upcoming game?
- How do you think about dropped catches and other errors?
- What filter do you bring when the selectors drop you from a team?
- Do you tend to be more pessimistic or optimistic?

To generate a more confident and composed mindset, replace the pessimistic words and phrases with sentences starting with: "I can...", "I will...", and "Yes and...."

Talk about your plans in terms of what, how and when. That will strengthen your mindset and resolve, which will help you to become the cricketer you want to be.

ACTIVITY 3: Be Grateful.

It's so easy to take for granted all the good things in our lives and to become absorbed in the one or two things that aren't going our way at the time. "Be Grateful" is a powerful and popular Mindfulness Practice used by people in all areas of life. It is a daily ritual of writing down three things for which you are grateful.

Instruction:

Here's a poignant example from a Player's Journal. Together with a bit of context, it provides a very clear example of how this simple tool can be applied for powerful results.

PLAYERS JOURNAL

In the past week I've been dropped from the team and last night I broke my index finger at practice, so at best I'm going to miss three games. My daily ritual is to write three things in my Journal for which I am grateful, so here goes:

I'm grateful my Mum is recovering from breast cancer.

I'm grateful that the break in my finger is a clean break.

I'm grateful for the support from my teammates.

When I spoke with the player, they said the entry about their Mum brought them to tears and helped put the whole thing in better perspective. That's a wonderful example of a Mindful Cricketer who is even stronger now because of what they've learned about themselves through facing down some tough situations.

REFLECTION QUESTIONS

Are you more naturally optimistic or pessimistic?

How is your current frame of mind helping or hindering your focus and execution of the game skills?

What thoughts and feelings cause mind drift towards the pessimistic?

How can you be quick to spot the triggers before things get out of control?

Is there an opportunity to use reframing more often in your day-to-day life?

Key Point Summary.

- Just as a camera takes different pictures depending on the filter over the lens, we see the world differently depending on the filters we use.
- If we bring a "pessimistic filter", chances are we'll be less confident, more stressed, and lower performing than if we choose an "optimistic filter".
- This distinction between optimism and pessimism is one of the strongest predictors of success in study, career and sport.
- Our own mistakes and our opponent's good luck have much less impact on whether we achieve our goals than what we do immediately after it happens.
- Build confidence, reduce anxiety and achieve better outcomes by framing situations with an optimistic mindset.
- Choose language and actions which reinforce an optimistic mindset.
- Be grateful.

Part D.

IMPLEMENTING THE GAME MINDSET FRAMEWORK

Building and Sharing.

The final section of *Mindful Cricket* brings together the pillars, principles and practices to set you up so you can implement this for yourself, your team or club.

This section is intentionally brief, because the content and approach continue to adapt and grow as our Mindful Cricket community creates and shares ideas and tools to bring the Game Mindset to life.

For the most up-to-date information on books, tools, drills and applications, or for online coaching and support, visit www.mindfulcricket.com.

CHAPTER 19

The Mindful Cricket Pathway.

Cricket is played above the shoulders. No one doubts that, but how do we learn to play that game?

A great place to start is by realising we play our best cricket (or do our best at anything) when mindful, which means our mind is clear, composed and fully focused on adapting to the challenges of the moment. However, we don't play so well when preoccupied with complicated thoughts, or distracted by impatience, self-doubt or even over-confidence.

The pathway to implementing Mindful Cricket is the Game Mindset which aims to do away with unhelpful and at times self-damaging practices, and instead to equip you with the mindset you need to be the best cricketer you can be.

Top athletes, teams and coaches around the world (from NBA stars, to Wimbledon champions and Olympic medallists) have embraced Mindful Practices as an integral part of their training and development, so this is a path well-trodden. However, those sports haven't had to grapple with the challenge of a competition environment, which is so different to the practice conditions.

Mindful Cricket brings those mindful practices together with insights from performance psychology - including adaptive thinking - to challenge and potentially change the way cricketers practise, prepare and play the game.

Game Mindset Framework.

The moment we step into the nets or onto the ground, we face **four universal enemies** that not only cause us to under-perform as cricketers, but also to be less than we want to be in other aspects of our life:

- Reactive mind - losing composure and letting unhelpful emotions take over
- Distraction and Mind Drift - being distracted from the present in the moments that matter
- Making it complicated - overthinking instead of keeping it simple
- Slow to change - being slow and inflexible to learn and adapt to change.

Observe players who are battling these enemies. Batsmen seem rushed and off balance, bowlers are straining and spraying deliveries, and fielders look ragged and disorganised. They're out of control of their own space and the shape of their actions.

Clear Mind.

There is enormous value in recognising these four universal enemies because they reveal **the principles and practices to defeat them** by fostering a Clear Mind:

1. **Cultivate composure** to calm the reactive mind
2. **Focus in the moment** to avoid distraction and mind drift
3. **Keep it simple** to cure complexity
4. **Adapt fast** to break out of slowness and inflexibility.

Observe players with a Clear Mind: they look organised and fluent in their set up and in their actions. They feel comfortable and in control of their game. They are owning their space and holding their shape, because that's what a Clear Mind enables them to do.

Blue Zone.

We instinctively know these foundation principles and practices are right because our experience of the blue performance zone is one of composure, focus, simplicity and adaptability.

It is there already! The blue zone is your unique Game Mindset, and from it you can learn what triggers you or blocks you from experiencing being comfortable and confident in your own game.

A Clear Mind will always be a key, but there are other elements to build on that clarity of mind: Play Brave, Play Clever, Play Better.

Play Brave tackles the fear of failure and doubt which creep into our minds, causing us to give up or even self-sabotage despite knowing we can be stronger and more powerful.

Play Clever is a rallying cry against dumb cricket. It is bringing your cricket smarts and using them to absorb and apply pressure to shape the momentum rather than letting it shape you - mindful not mindless.

Play Better is a mindset of always learning and growing, and of optimism underpinned by daily habits that build reliable consistency in your game instead of random highs and lows.

The Game Mindset Framework is simple and suggests more than just a way to play cricket. Clear Mind, Play Brave, Play Clever, Play Better is a call to action you can apply in sport, study, career and life.

Where to From Here?

How can you use the simple practices and tools of Game Mindset to have the greatest possible impact on your own cricket enjoyment and performance, or use it to coach others? My suggestion is:

1. Complete the Mindful Cricket book and engage regularly at www. mindfulcricket.com, where you will find all sorts of resources and support to implement the principles, practices and activities.
2. Follow the five-step pathway in the next section and use practices like PDCA in net sessions to accelerate your learning and improvement.

3. If you want a helping hand, then check in for some online coaching until you build your own momentum to create the breakthrough you want.

Five Steps Along the Pathway.

From my experience, there are five steps which players and coaches find most effective in implementing the Game Mindset framework, and the good news is you are ready now to put them into place, provided you are willing to devote time to achieve the benefits:

1. Know Your Blue Zone
2. Cultivate Composure
3. Focus in the Moment
4. Keep it Simple, and Adapt Fast
5. Choose Your Priorities.

STEP 1: Know Your Blue Zone.

The blue zone is the place to really get to know, because it reveals the blueprint for your unique Game Mindset, while reinforcing the value of a Clear Mind and Playing Brave, Playing Clever and Playing Better.

Devote time to do the 'Find Your Performance Zone' activity. Observe and explore the shifts in your mindset as the zones change for you. For example, be aware how the red zone makes things seem to move faster and be more complicated, whereas the blue zone brings composure and focus which seems to naturally quell the reactive mind and distractions. Be aware how this affects your game, whether you are batting, bowling, fielding or keeping. This awareness lays the ideal foundation, because all the work you put in on Game Mindset is designed to get you into the blue zone.

STEP 2: Cultivate Composure.

When asked which pillar or practice is most important in Game Mindset, my preference is to refer back to the game of chess and the two most important pieces: the king and the queen.

Composure is king, because without composure the reactive mind is in charge, and that damages everything else. So, begin with Composure and choose a Mindful Practice which helps to develop your Centred Breathing and calming skills. Find time each day to practise creating the stillness, and quiet observation of your breathing, that will pay big dividends in those moments that matter.

STEP 3: Focus in the Moment.

If Composure is king in our game of chess, then Focus in the Moment is queen, because that's where the power of mindfulness is unlocked. When we truly stay in the moment, we play our best without getting in our own way or letting things outside our control detract from performance.

If there is one practice to prioritise to support this principle, it is 1-2-3 Reset. It builds on Composure and fits perfectly into your cricket repertoire in a natural and valuable way, because every delivery needs a switch on or reset.

STEP 4: Keep it Simple and Adapt Fast.

If we continue our chess analogy, the next pieces to move are Keep it Simple and Adapt Fast. Think of these together because both are fundamentally about the Learning Loop - the power of the ritual of Plan, Do, Check and Adapt.

Your choice here depends on how serious you are about embracing Mindful Cricket as a way of life. If you are deep diving, then consider creating a Performance Planning Space and committing to using the PDCA Learning Loop in weekly sprints, because that's a potential game changer.

At any level, I strongly recommend using PDCA at practice and combining it with a Go-To-Plan, because that's a great way to create a more match-like practice mindset and environment.

STEP 5: Choose Your Priorities.

With those foundations in place, the next move is yours to choose from the other nine principles:

Play Brave	Play Clever	Play Better
Create Your Bold Vision	Bat Smart	Apply A Growth Mindset
Put it on the Line	Bowl Smart	Be Game Ready
Hold the Tension	Keep and Field Smart	Bring Optimism

Each principle has examples of practices and activities in the book, and the Workbook, and more are available online as we continue to build on ideas from the Mindful Cricket community.

Resources and Support.

My hope in writing *Mindful Cricket* is for the book and the accompanying Mindful Cricket Workbook to be just the starting point on a journey of helping cricketers and coaches to gain more enjoyment and success from the game.

At www.mindfulcricket.com you will find a range of resources and links to articles, tools and courses.

For coaches and clubs there will be continuing resources to support our Coaching Mindful Cricket and Leading Mindful Cricket programs. The latter draw on resources and approaches we have developed at Think One Team Consulting www.thinkoneteam.com to help enterprises to set up their leadership teams and to foster an agile and adaptive way of operating.

A Final Word.

Cricket is a wonderful sport which prepares us all for the wider challenges of life. It can be maddeningly frustrating during a run of bad form, or wildly exhilarating when we win as a team or achieve a personal milestone.

Perhaps the greatest beauty of cricket is where and how it is played. I've been fortunate to travel and watch cricket played with all manner of equipment in courtyards in Sri Lanka, in fields and on beaches in India, on manicured grounds in England and the Middle East, and in stadiums in Australia and New Zealand. On occasions I've glimpsed cricket in Malaysia, Singapore and Nepal, in Holland and Canada, and on a dusty road near the India-Pakistan border.

No matter where you play and with what equipment, it is always a game played above the shoulders. While cricket prepares us for life, I hope Mindful Cricket and the simplicity of the Game Mindset help prepare you to bring to the great game a Clear Mind and the attitude to Play Brave, Play Clever and Play Better.

Because that's the mindset you need to be the best cricketer you can be.

Good luck and good cricket.

References.

Bishop, SR 2004, 'Mindfulness: A Proposed Operational Definition', *Clinical Psychology*, vol. 11, no. 3, pp. 230-241.

Brown, B 2015, *Rising Strong (First Edition)*, Random House, New York.

D'Anello, L 2019, 'Dhoni lauded by Australian peers', *cricket.com.au*, 10 January, viewed 15 February 2019, <https://www.cricket.com.au/news/ms-dhoni-wins-praise-from-australian-counterparts-india-odi-series-tim-paine-pat-cummins/2019-01-10>

Dweck, CS 2008, *Mindset: The New Psychology of Success*, Ballantine Books, New York.

ESPNCricinfo Staff, 2016, "Emotional' Kohli rates Mohali knock his best', *ESPNcricinfo*, 27 March, viewed 15 February 2019, <http://www.espncricinfo.com/icc-world-twenty20-2016/content/story/991795.html>

Ferriss, T., 2007, *The 4-Hour Workweek: Escape 9-5, Live anywhere, and join the New Rich*, Crown Publishing Group.

Gallwey, WT 1979, *The Inner Game of Tennis*, Bantam Books, Toronto.

Gawande, A 2010, *The Checklist Manifesto: How to Get Things Right*, Metropolitan Books, New York.

Kabat-Zinn, J 1994, *Wherever You Go, There You Are: Mindfulness Meditation in Everyday Life*, Hyperion Books, New York.

Roosevelt, T 1910, *Citizenship in a Republic*, 23 April, Sorbonne, Paris.

Tolle, E 1997, *The Power of Now: A Guide to Spiritual Enlightenment*, Namaste Publishing, Vancouver.